The Firewall Whisperer: Palo Alt aster Prevention Device

Table of Contents
"PANorama of Protection: 25 Chapters Through the Palo Alto IDS Time Tunnel"

- More memory, faster inspection, and deeper packet analysis.
- Supported the early WildFire threat detection add-ons.
- Required space, airflow, and understanding spouses.

Chapter 7: PA-4060 – The Refined Dinosaur
- Tuned IDS/IPS performance with better stability.
- Admins finally stopped yelling at the CLI.
- Not quite modern, not quite forgotten.

Chapter 8: PA-5020 – Data Center Entry Level
- Stepped up for large organizations with better DPI.
- IDS services worked *while* managing traffic.
- Finally proved Palo Alto wasn't just for SMBs.

Chapter 9: PA-5050 – Speed and Signatures, Together at Last
- Efficient threat prevention and faster SSL decryption.
- Made data center IDS feel less like a gamble.
- Still in service where people forget to upgrade.

Chapter 10: PA-5060 – The OG Titan
- Palo Alto's muscle box for serious enterprise security.
- Consistent IDS/IPS under heavy traffic—finally!
- Needed a dedicated rack and a whispered apology to your power bill.

Chapter 11: PA-3020 – The Midrange Marvel
- Balanced price, performance, and App-ID IDS.
- A hit in education and healthcare networks.
- Still holding the fort in places that think "cloud" is weather.

Chapter 12: PA-3050 – The MVP of Mid-Sized IDS
- IDS/IPS scanning with smarter signature handling.
- Ran PAN-OS 8.x without breaking a sweat (usually).
- Survived years of admins pushing it "just one more upgrade."

Chapter 13: PA-3060 – IDS Meets Intelligence
- Best of the 3000s, optimized for serious security work.
- Supported advanced threat services and more sessions.
- Secretly everyone's favorite underdog.

Chapter 14: PA-7080 – The First Behemoth

- Chassis-style modular IDS system with scary power.
- Replaced clusters of smaller devices with one monster.
- Scared attackers—and IT budgets.

Chapter 15: PA-220 – Cute, Quiet, and Competent
- Remote office IDS with PAN-OS power in a lunchbox.
- Sleek enough for desks, strong enough for branches.
- Great cost-to-protection ratio (if you didn't throw too much at it).

Chapter 16: PA-820 – The Goldilocks Box
- Branch/SMB IDS that handled modern threats gracefully.
- Replaced aging PA-500s without the fan rage.
- Better hardware acceleration and App-ID enhancements.

Chapter 17: PA-850 – Compact with a Kick
- IDS with turbo—great for busy branch offices.
- Improved SSL decryption and WildFire integration.
- Underestimated until it caught something nasty.

Chapter 18: PA-3220 – The Modern Middleweight
- Designed for midsize orgs entering cloud hybrid territory.
- Deep IDS visibility and traffic analysis without meltdown.
- Survived 2020 traffic spikes with grace.

Chapter 19: PA-3250 – Midrange Hero Mode Activated
- Better memory and compute for signature-heavy environments.
- Faster threat detection and streamlined logging.
- Often deployed with zero regrets.

Chapter 20: PA-3260 – IDS for the Evolving Edge
- High-speed detection without needing a forklift.
- Ideal for growing companies that outpaced their PA-3050s.
- Liked by auditors, tolerated by budget committees.

Chapter 21: PA-5220 – The Data Center Defender
- Enterprise IDS with more cores, smarter filtering.
- Tuned for threat detection with serious uptime needs.
- The box that said "yes" when the others said "wait."

Chapter 22: PA-5250 – Speed, Space, and Security

- Deeper traffic inspection at faster speeds.
- Loved by cloud integrators and large compliance teams.
- Ran PAN-OS 10.x like butter on toast.

Chapter 23: PA-5260 – Because Gigabit Isn't Enough
- Big bandwidth meets smarter IDS/IPS correlation.
- Sailed through inspection tasks others choked on.
- Datacenter favorite, if you had enough rack space.

Chapter 24: PA-5450 – The Flagship Phoenix
- Newer, leaner, hotter version of its 5200 ancestors.
- Supports modern ML-based detection and TLS 1.3 inspection.
- Built for hybrid clouds, data lakes, and big dreams.

Chapter 25: PA-7530 – Apex Predator in the PAN Jungle
- Next-gen modular box with ML-powered IDS.
- SecOps-friendly with real-time threat behavior modeling.
- For when compromise is not an option (or financially possible).

Chapter 1: PA-200 – The Network Gnome

1.

Meet the PA-200, the tiniest warrior in the Palo Alto arsenal. It's not big, flashy, or particularly loud, but this palm-sized protector has the heart of a lion and the patience of a saint. Designed for small offices and remote sites, it's your go-to firewall when space is limited and security isn't negotiable. If it were a Dungeons & Dragons character, it'd be a rogue gnome—quiet, clever, and way more dangerous than it looks. Don't let its size fool you; this little box is all business.

2.

The PA-200 isn't trying to win a data center brawl. Instead, it thrives in tight spaces, home offices, and small branches where performance needs are modest but uptime and security are mission-critical. It handles up to 100 Mbps of firewall throughput, which for the average small business is more than enough to keep traffic flowing and threats at bay. Think of it as the IT equivalent of a very competent butler—polite, efficient, and somehow always one step ahead of trouble.

3.

Under the hood, the PA-200 sports a dual-core processor and 512 MB of RAM. Not exactly what you'd call muscular, but like a caffeine-fueled squirrel, it gets the job done with agility. It runs PAN-OS, the same operating system as its bigger siblings, which means it brings the same brain even if it can't lift as much. It's like having a genius in a Fiat Panda—small ride, big IQ.

4.

Physically, the PA-200 comes with four 10/100/1000 Ethernet ports and a sleek, fanless design. The fanless aspect is crucial for quiet environments like executive offices or remote closets where buzz is frowned upon. It's passive-cooled, meaning it's silent—unless you count the whisper of packets being scanned. It's basically the librarian of the network world: silent, disciplined, and terrifyingly effective.

5.

Zero noise, low heat, and no moving parts also means higher durability. Fewer mechanical components equal fewer failure points. This gnome might not lift heavy logs, but it also doesn't throw its back out. Its silent endurance is great for long-haul deployments in dusty wiring closets or "temporary" offices that have mysteriously lasted seven years.

6.

You get the full suite of Palo Alto security features: App-ID, User-ID, Content-ID, and WildFire integration. Yes, even in this budget-friendly unit. It's like buying a compact car that somehow still comes with satellite navigation, heated seats, and a holographic dashboard. Small doesn't mean stripped-down; the PA-200 has the brains and behavior analysis of the big boys.

7.

App-ID lets it recognize traffic based on applications, not ports. So even if someone decides to tunnel BitTorrent traffic over port 80 (sneaky devils), the PA-200 sees right through it. It's like having Sherlock Holmes stationed at your branch office network gateway. "Ah yes, that's not HTTPS… that's Minecraft cloaked in TCP."

8.

User-ID ties traffic to actual user identities, not just IP addresses. That means no more chasing ghost IPs when tracking suspicious activity—"Who's 192.168.1.45?" becomes "Oh, it's Dave from Accounting again." With Active Directory, LDAP, and a sprinkle of LDAP magic, the PA-200 gives you meaningful visibility into who is doing what.

9.

Content-ID is the PA-200's in-line digital sniffer dog. It scans for threats, viruses, and data leaks with all the tenacity of a mall security guard who just found a kid skateboarding indoors. It blocks malware, prevents data exfiltration, and even stops inappropriate content. You won't need to explain to HR why the printer queue is full of cat memes again.

10.

Want threat intelligence from the cloud? Enter WildFire. Even this humble gnome can submit suspicious files to Palo Alto's cloud-based sandbox. Once detonated, those files get globally analyzed and tagged, and your PA-200 gets smarter in real-time. It's like your firewall took a night class in malware forensics and started applying it immediately.

11.

The management interface is classic Palo Alto—clean, web-based, and intuitive. You don't need a PhD in CLI gymnastics to configure this thing. GUI purists and command-line warriors both have their paths to enlightenment. And if you want centralized control, it integrates beautifully with Panorama for fleet-wide policy pushes.

12.

Speaking of Panorama, the PA-200 plays nice with its older siblings in distributed environments. A branch office here, a retail outlet there—hook them all to a central Panorama and manage security policies like a benevolent overlord. It's like having one brain controlling many arms, and each arm has an IDS/IPS baked in.

13.

The PA-200 also supports virtual wire mode, Layer 2 and Layer 3 deployments. Whether you want to do transparent bump-in-the-wire filtering or route traffic like a proper gateway, it's got you covered. Its flexibility is unmatched for its size, like a Swiss Army knife in firewall form.

14.

It supports HA (High Availability) in active/passive mode. Yep, even this little nugget can participate in redundancy. Two PA-200s can form a tiny, adorable HA pair that's ready to pick up where the other left off if one gets unplugged by the janitor. They're like firewalls in friendship bracelets—always got each other's back.

15.

Logs and reports? Of course. The PA-200 keeps detailed logs and can generate alerts, summaries, and granular traffic reports. It doesn't just guard your perimeter—it gives you a PowerPoint-ready explanation of what it did last night while you were asleep. Managers love it. Auditors worship it.

16.

Performance-wise, you get around 100 Mbps of firewall throughput, 50 Mbps of threat prevention, and about 20,000 max sessions. Sure, it won't win a speed test at a data center LAN party, but for a 5–10 user branch office or retail kiosk, it's plenty. The real magic is in consistent, reliable protection without unexpected slowdowns.

17.

It also supports IPsec VPNs and SSL VPNs for secure remote connectivity. Road warriors, remote offices, and teleworkers can tunnel in safely and securely. Combine this with GlobalProtect and boom—you have a tiny, travel-friendly security gateway that's got your back from Bangkok to Baltimore.

18.

The PA-200 may not have flashy SFP ports or multiple 10G interfaces, but what it lacks in horsepower it makes up for in reliability and simplicity. It's the Toyota Corolla of firewalls—low maintenance, hard to kill, and surprisingly useful in most situations. It also doesn't complain when you ask it to do overtime.

19.

When it comes to updates, the PA-200 receives the same threat signatures and dynamic updates as every other Palo Alto firewall. No class divide here—it gets the same security intelligence as the PA-7080 in a Fortune 100 data center. Think of it as a network hobbit with access to elven weaponry.

20.

You can even do captive portal and SSL decryption, although you may want to be selective depending on your performance needs. It'll do it, just don't ask it to decrypt the entire Netflix catalog during lunch hour. Pick your battles, and this little guy will win them.

21.

Environmentally conscious? The PA-200 draws under 15 watts. That's about as much power as a fancy LED desk lamp. Great for reducing your branch's carbon footprint—or at least keeping the electric bill low enough for another pot of breakroom coffee.

22.

This firewall is also a dream for MSPs and consultants. Easy to ship, deploy, and manage remotely. With ZTP (Zero Touch Provisioning) and cloud-delivered configurations, you can spin up protection without ever setting foot in Boise. Or Peoria. Or that one remote dentist office with a raccoon problem.

23.

For training purposes, it's also a beloved lab toy. Students and instructors alike appreciate having a real-deal PAN-OS device to learn on. The PA-200 might not break benchmarks, but it'll build firewall experts who can. It's the dojo master of small firewalls.

24.

End-of-life? Sadly, yes—the PA-200 has entered retirement mode, but many are still in operation and kicking. If you're managing legacy deployments, understanding this model is still crucial. And hey, there's something charming about a firewall that still works after ten years of service and three moves.

25.

In the grand story of Palo Alto's IDS/IPS evolution, the PA-200 is the unassuming hero who held the line when no one else could. It didn't need fame or fanfare. It just needed power, a cat5 cable, and a chance to prove itself. And prove itself, it did—one silent packet inspection at a time.

Chapter 2: PA-500 – Small Office, Big Aspirations

1.

Welcome the PA-500, the firewall equivalent of an overachieving intern who shows up early, stays late, and somehow knows more than your IT manager. Designed for small to medium offices, it's the next logical step when the PA-200 starts wheezing under packet pressure. If the PA-200 is a network gnome, the PA-500 is its taller, stronger cousin who went to community college and got *certified*.

2.

Physically, the PA-500 is rack-mountable, sleek, and about the size of a large pizza box— because enterprise-grade security deserves proper toppings. It comes equipped with 10 Ethernet ports: eight for data (RJ-45) and two for high-availability (HA1/HA2). That's right—this little beast is ready for teamwork. HA pairs unite!

3.

Under the metal, you get more RAM, more CPU, and more ambition. The PA-500 sports a 1.8 GHz dual-core processor and up to 2 GB of RAM, depending on revision. It may not be benching server racks, but it can definitely do pushups with policies strapped to its back.

4.

Performance-wise, it delivers up to 250 Mbps of firewall throughput and 100 Mbps of threat prevention. Not quite carrier-grade, but more than enough to secure small business traffic, cloud apps, VoIP calls, and the occasional questionable Google search. It's the IDS/IPS equivalent of a sprinter with a clipboard.

5.

The PA-500 runs PAN-OS, just like its big brothers, and yes — it supports App-ID, User-ID, Content-ID, and WildFire. Every bit of Palo Alto's secret sauce is in here. No watered-down version, no missing ingredients. If the PA-500 were soup, it would be chowder — thick, rich, and a little spicy.

6.

App-ID ensures your firewall isn't just guessing what traffic is — it knows. Is that port 443 carrying encrypted email or a clandestine Fortnite update? The PA-500 knows. It's like hiring an app psychic who can peer into packets and say, "That's not Teams, my friend — that's Steam."

7.

User-ID means you know who's doing what, not just what's being done. No more hunting down devices by MAC addresses like a networking episode of *CSI*. Tie traffic to real users via AD, LDAP, or local accounts. It's user-centric policy enforcement, and it's glorious.

8.

With Content-ID, the PA-500 blocks viruses, malware, spyware, and suspicious payloads. It can filter URLs, inspect SSL traffic (if enabled), and scan for sensitive data leaks. Think of it as a data bouncer — firm but fair, with a clipboard full of denial messages.

9.

Want to sandbox a suspicious file? No problem — WildFire integration is baked in. The PA-500 can send unknown executables, PDFs, and other files to Palo Alto's cloud sandbox to detonate and analyze. If the file explodes, your network stays safe. It's a "blow up first, ask questions later" kind of policy — and it works.

10.

Deployment options are varied: virtual wire (transparent), Layer 2, or Layer 3. Whether you want it as a bridge, a switch, or a full-on router with IDS/IPS goggles, the PA-500 adapts like a networking chameleon. Just don't ask it to play your Spotify.

11.

The PA-500 includes management via web UI, CLI, and centralized Panorama support. Web GUI is intuitive, responsive, and polished — like the firewall equivalent of a good résumé. CLI access gives hardcore admins what they need to script, grep, and automate like they mean it.

12.

You can define granular security policies, set threat profiles, and apply URL filtering with surgical precision. You want all interns blocked from YouTube during office hours? Done. You want HR exempted? Also done. You want to see who's secretly watching cooking videos at 2 p.m.? Easy.

13.

SSL decryption is supported, albeit with moderate performance impact. It's great for enforcing policies within encrypted traffic—but remember, the PA-500 isn't a decrypting speed demon. It's more like a cryptographic tortoise: slow, steady, and secure.

14.

Logging is extensive, detailed, and timestamped with forensic perfection. You can export logs, set up syslog forwarding, and even integrate with SIEMs for that "enterprise feel" in a smaller package. The PA-500 takes its documentation duties seriously—it's the nerd who takes notes during meetings.

15.

You've got VPN support, too. Both IPsec and SSL VPNs are on the table. That means your remote employees, satellite offices, or disgruntled database admins on vacation in Aruba can all connect securely. Bonus points if they remember their pre-shared key.

16.

HA support? Yes—active/passive failover is available. When one PA-500 dies valiantly in battle, the other picks up the shield and charges forward. Your network stays protected. Your boss doesn't scream. And you look like a redundancy rockstar.

17.

Worried about updates? Don't be. You get the same threat and application signature updates as the high-end models. You're not left out just because you bought the budget-friendly model. The PA-500 reads the same cybersecurity headlines as the PA-7080—just with less caffeine.

18.

The PA-500's fan-assisted cooling is audible but not annoying. You'll hear a low hum when it's working hard, like a network monk meditating in your server closet. It may be small, but it hums with purpose.

19.

It draws more power than the PA-200, averaging around 45 watts, but that's still remarkably low. Your electric bill won't spike, and you'll still have money for office snacks—which, let's face it, is how you really win over the team.

20.

It supports captive portal, custom block pages, and authentication policies that let you control access with style. Want your users to log in before browsing? Want to brand the block page with a dancing taco? Be my guest. The PA-500's got flair.

21.

Retail branches, law offices, real estate firms, and regional offices have all found their match in the PA-500. It's secure enough for compliance, flexible enough for growth, and quiet enough to keep your Zen. Even your accountant will love it—especially during tax season.

22.

One of the best use cases? Remote locations that still require enterprise-grade control. Think executive home offices, retail chains, or that one sales office with six people and a love of cat GIFs. The PA-500 handles it with grace.

23.

It's also a great entry point for IT teams looking to introduce Palo Alto Networks to their organization. Easy to deploy, easy to learn, and easy to love. It's the firewall version of a first date that actually calls you back.

24.

The PA-500 is now end-of-sale, but many are still active in production networks. If you're inheriting one or maintaining legacy deployments, keep your PAN-OS up to date and give it the care it deserves. Just because it's retired doesn't mean it's irrelevant.

25.

In the big family of Palo Alto firewalls, the PA-500 is the middle child that figured out how to get noticed—by doing its job flawlessly. It doesn't crave attention, but it gets results. If your office dreams of enterprise-grade security but only has a startup-sized budget, this was—and in some cases, still is—the perfect fit.

Chapter 3: PA-2020 – The Beeping Midrange Beginnings

1.

Say hello to the PA-2020—the Palo Alto that kicked off midrange ambitions with a sense of purpose and, occasionally, a little too much beeping. This was the box that said, "I'm not small anymore," while still trying to find its footing in the adult firewall world. If the PA-200 was a gnome and the PA-500 was a college grad, the PA-2020 is a newly promoted middle manager with a Bluetooth headset and a lot to prove.

2.

The PA-2020 arrived with 10 Gigabit Ethernet ports and all the seriousness of a firewall trying to break into the enterprise scene. With dedicated management and HA ports, it was the first of its kind to flirt with real traffic handling muscle—though more of a treadmill than a powerlifter. It looked sharp, felt capable, and, oh yes, it beeped. Loudly. Often. For reasons sometimes only it understood.

3.

At the core, the PA-2020 was built on x86 architecture, housing a dual-core processor and 4 GB of RAM. That might not sound like much now, but back then, it felt like strapping a rocket to a firewall the size of a pizza box. And that memory? Used wisely by PAN-OS to juggle inspection, logging, session tracking, and the occasional bout of existential questioning.

4.

Firewall throughput was rated at up to 500 Mbps, with threat prevention around 250 Mbps. For SMBs and small enterprises, this was more than enough to guard against malware, botnets, and that one intern who insists on torrenting Linux ISOs during lunch. It may not win the 100-meter dash, but it could definitely run a half-marathon without collapsing.

5.

What made the PA-2020 a real player was that it ran the full PAN-OS suite. You got App-ID, Content-ID, User-ID, and WildFire support in a chassis that didn't scream "branch office." It had all the features of the big iron, just in a slightly louder box with a bit less horsepower and significantly more sass.

6.

App-ID on the PA-2020 meant real application awareness. Not just "port 80 means web," but "that's Facebook, and that's Zoom, and yes, Dave from Legal is watching TikToks during meetings." It classified traffic based on behavior and not assumptions, which was kind of revolutionary for a box this size.

7.

User-ID integration gave it context—"Who is doing what, not just what is being done." By syncing with Active Directory, LDAP, or local databases, it tagged traffic with usernames. So, when a suspicious download happened, you weren't looking at an IP—you were staring at Brenda from HR's digital fingerprints.

8.

Content-ID, as always, did the heavy lifting on threat detection and prevention. It blocked viruses, scanned for spyware, sniffed out command-and-control traffic, and made sure nobody emailed the company's secret BBQ sauce recipe outside the firewall. It even filtered adult content, which meant the PA-2020 helped keep your office PG-rated, 24/7.

9.

And yes, WildFire was supported. The PA-2020 could submit unknown files to Palo Alto's cloud sandbox for dynamic analysis. Suspicious files were detonated in a virtual environment far away from your network, keeping your systems clean and your productivity intact. WildFire on a PA-2020 was like giving a Boy Scout a flamethrower—with strict rules.

10.

Deployment modes included virtual wire, Layer 2, and Layer 3. Want it transparent? No problem. Want it routing and NATing like a pro? Done. This box could fit in anywhere, like a network Swiss Army knife with extra firewall blades.

11.

Logging was extensive, and the reporting interface was standard Palo Alto: web-based, polished, and very manager-friendly. If your boss wanted graphs, pie charts, or a report that looked impressive enough for a board meeting, the PA-2020 had your back. Just don't tell them you generated it during lunch.

12.

High Availability support? Absolutely. You could pair two PA-2020s in active/passive mode. That meant one unit could go up in smoke (figuratively—or literally, depending on cable management), and the other would take over without missing a packet. It was firewall friendship at its finest.

13.

SSL decryption was possible, though you had to manage expectations. This unit could inspect encrypted traffic, but don't expect it to deep-dive into every HTTPS stream without some performance dips. Choose wisely: decrypt only the important stuff (like file uploads), not Grandma's cookie blog.

14.

The management interface included a dedicated Ethernet port and CLI access via console. Whether you were a GUI enthusiast or a CLI purist, the PA-2020 let you have your cake and configure it, too. You could SSH in and feel like a wizard—or click buttons like a modern-day general.

15.

It supported all the expected enterprise features: static routes, OSPF, BGP, DHCP, NAT, and policy-based forwarding. The PA-2020 wasn't just a filter; it was a full-fledged network appliance. Your network could be complex—this box was built to understand that complexity and secure it.

16.

On the physical side, it had front-facing ports, status LEDs, and—brace yourself—a very enthusiastic beeper. Alerts, warnings, HA failures, memory issues? Beep. Sometimes it beeped just to remind you it was alive. Admins got used to it. Some even developed a Pavlovian response.

17.

Cooling was active, with fans that kept it comfortably under thermal limits. Unlike its fanless cousins, the PA-2020 wasn't silent—but at least it wasn't trying to whisper secrets through its heatsink. It said, "I'm working," and made sure you knew it.

18.

Power draw was moderate, sitting around 70–90 watts depending on load. Not exactly eco-friendly, but not server-grade either. It wouldn't double your utility bill, but it might make you think twice about stacking five of them in a closet with no airflow.

19.

From a licensing perspective, you had all the usual suspects: Threat Prevention, URL Filtering, WildFire, GlobalProtect, and Premium Support. Budget-conscious admins often started with

Threat Prevention and WildFire—because really, malware and unknown files were the bad guys in 99% of use cases.

20.

VPN? Absolutely. The PA-2020 supported IPsec site-to-site and remote access VPNs. SSL VPN was there, too, and with GlobalProtect, mobile users could connect securely from coffee shops, airports, and suspicious hotel Wi-Fi with all the paranoia of a trained infosec analyst.

21.

When used in Panorama-managed environments, the PA-2020 became part of a much bigger, smarter whole. Centralized logging, global policy pushes, and real-time threat visibility—like giving your firewall a hive mind. Suddenly, even this midrange model was playing in the enterprise league.

22.

Despite being discontinued, the PA-2020 still shows up in production networks, particularly in educational, healthcare, and legal environments where budget meets necessity. If yours is still running, treat it kindly. Update its firmware. Clean its fans. Let it beep its way to legacy glory.

23.

This model paved the way for future midrange marvels like the PA-3020 and PA-820. It was the stepping stone from "starter firewalls" to "serious security infrastructure." And for many admins, it was their first hands-on experience with Palo Alto hardware. Nostalgia included.

24.

One of its quirks—aside from its occasional beep serenades—was its tendency to fill its internal log partition quickly if not properly managed. Best practice? Forward logs to Panorama or a syslog server. Otherwise, it'd start grumbling and, you guessed it… beeping.

25.

The PA-2020 may be retired, but it lives on as a milestone. It proved that midrange firewalls didn't have to be compromises—they could be complete packages with enterprise DNA. It protected businesses, connected users, and made a whole generation of IT folks flinch every time they heard a random beep. And for that, we salute it.

Chapter 4: PA-2050 – Older Sibling Energy

1.

Meet the PA-2050: the firewall that walks into the server room, sees the PA-2020 struggling with a full packet queue, and says, "Step aside, little bro." This is Palo Alto's elder statesman of midrange protection—a device with broader shoulders, deeper logs, and the kind of "been there, blocked that" energy only older siblings understand. It came out swinging with more ports, more performance, and the same PAN-OS brain.

2.

Physically, the PA-2050 looks nearly identical to the 2020, but under the hood, it's packing more firepower. Twelve Gigabit Ethernet ports (10 data, 2 HA) sit across the front like a row of confident firewall teeth. And like every older sibling at a family BBQ, it knows how to multitask while pretending it's not stressed.

3.

We're talking throughput now — 1 Gbps of firewall horsepower. That's double the 2020. Threat prevention clocks in at 500 Mbps, giving the 2050 plenty of muscle for medium-sized offices, schools, or branch locations that do more than just browse the web and argue over who ordered lunch.

4.

At the heart of this beast is a stronger CPU, more memory (4 GB RAM and 80 GB SSD), and a chipset that knows how to handle multitasking like a pro. Whether it's routing, inspecting SSL, or screaming silently when a user downloads malware for the third time today, the PA-2050 holds its ground.

5.

Of course, it runs PAN-OS, because what's a Palo Alto firewall without its crown jewel? That means App-ID, Content-ID, User-ID, and WildFire are all included — no "lite" version, no stripped-down nonsense. This firewall comes fully loaded and emotionally mature.

6.

App-ID is your application bouncer, trained to recognize traffic by behavior, not by port. The 2050 can sniff out YouTube over port 443, Dropbox inside HTTPS, or your intern's "important research" session that's really Netflix in disguise. If applications were party crashers, this firewall is the velvet rope.

7.

User-ID integrates seamlessly with Active Directory, giving your firewall the power of name recognition. No more hunting anonymous IPs — now it's "Kyle from Marketing is hammering Reddit again," and yes, policies can be tied directly to Kyle. He's going to learn today.

8.

Content-ID brings the thunder. Antivirus, anti-spyware, data loss prevention, file blocking, and URL filtering all packed into one tight feature set. The PA-2050 can stop threats in real-time while reporting exactly who tried to exfiltrate the company's "Super Secret Project" folder to Google Drive.

9.

WildFire integration gives it cloud-powered threat analysis, meaning the PA-2050 not only blocks known threats, it helps discover unknown ones. It's like the FBI's cyber division on a flash drive — minus the paperwork and drama. Detonate suspicious files in a virtual lab and share intel globally in minutes.

10.

VPN support? You bet. Site-to-site IPsec VPNs, SSL remote access with GlobalProtect — everything an office needs to stay connected securely. Whether it's a retail store, a satellite campus, or someone's overly enthusiastic home lab, the 2050 keeps tunnels tight and safe.

11.

Deployment is flexible. Use it in Layer 3, Layer 2, or virtual wire mode depending on your topology and spiritual alignment. Got MPLS? Cool. Need to drop it in transparently between a sketchy switch and your uplink? Even better. The PA-2050 adapts like a network ninja.

12.

High Availability comes standard, with full active/passive capabilities. Pair two 2050s and you've got yourself a fault-tolerant fortress. One goes down, the other kicks in like a caffeine-fueled sysadmin with a pager. No missed packets. No downtime. No drama.

13.

SSL decryption is here, too, although you'll want to be judicious. This model can decrypt and inspect HTTPS traffic, but don't go crazy trying to decrypt a campus's worth of YouTube at once. Think surgical scalpel, not sledgehammer—use policies to target the high-risk stuff.

14.

Logs? Oh, the logs. Detailed, timestamped, searchable, exportable. The PA-2050 documents everything it sees with the accuracy of a detective's notebook and the verbosity of a first-year lit major. Tie in Panorama and your centralized logging dreams come true.

15.

You also get a dedicated management port, a console port, and intuitive web-based GUI access. CLI fans aren't left behind either—you can SSH in and script to your heart's content. Whether you click or type, the 2050's ready to let you configure policies in your preferred style.

16.

On the subject of policies, you get full next-gen control: application-based rules, user-based permissions, time-based access, and the legendary Palo Alto security profiles. Want to allow Dropbox only for HR, only during business hours, and only after lunch? Yes. You can.

17.

Hardware-wise, it's active-cooled with a fan that hums with purpose—not loud, but noticeable. The PA-2050 likes to let you know it's working. It's the server room's white noise machine, blowing warm air and good vibes.

18.

Power draw sits around 150 watts under moderate load. It's no ultralight, but it's not a rack-scorcher either. With proper airflow, it stays chill. Just don't bury it under that one pile of unlabeled Cat6 cables everyone pretends isn't a fire hazard.

19.

SSL VPN capabilities through GlobalProtect allow remote workers to connect securely. With endpoint health checks and policy enforcement, you're not just letting people in—you're vetting them first. The 2050 is the bouncer with a clipboard *and* a black belt.

20.

Licensing options are familiar: Threat Prevention, WildFire, URL Filtering, GlobalProtect, and Premium Support. You pick your security flavor, and the PA-2050 delivers it hot. Some licenses unlock features; others just make your legal team sleep easier at night.

21.
Captive portal is available and customizable. Whether it's a redirect-to-login for guest Wi-Fi or a terms-and-conditions splash page with your company's logo and passive-aggressive branding, the 2050's got you. Great for retail, guest networks, or that one guy who always needs "just five more minutes."

22.
It supports role-based admin access and local or centralized authentication. Give read-only access to interns, full control to your network deity, and audit logs to your compliance overlords. No more "accidentally deleted a security rule" incidents. (Looking at you, Chad.)

23.
Still running in the wild? Oh yes. The PA-2050 might be end-of-sale, but it's still in racks across the world doing what it does best: keeping bad traffic out and good traffic flowing. It's not flashy. It's not trendy. But it's loyal, durable, and battle-tested.

24.
Its biggest limitation today is age—firmware support is slowly fading, and modern bandwidth demands are pushing its limits. But if you're running one today, know that it paved the way for beasts like the PA-3200 series. It's a firewall with war stories, and it earned those scars.

25.
The PA-2050 was, and still is in many networks, the dependable older sibling of Palo Alto's early generations. It came with more power, more ports, and a protective streak. It beeped less than the 2020 (thankfully), blocked more, and helped define what midrange IDS/IPS could be. If it had a motto, it'd be: "I've got this." And for years, it did.

Chapter 5: PA-4020 – The Gateway to Enterprise Firepower

1.
Behold the PA-4020: the first Palo Alto firewall that could walk into a data center, shake hands with a Cisco core switch, and say, "I belong here." This wasn't a small office box. This was Palo Alto flexing its muscles—an enterprise-grade, rack-hogging, bandwidth-wrangling beast that officially declared, "We do more than branches now."

2.
The PA-4020 is part of Palo Alto's original 4000 Series—built for the enterprise but without requiring a forklift or a cloud architect to run it. It's like a middle manager who somehow bench-presses 1Gbps while filling out compliance reports. With a 2U chassis, front-facing fans, and an unmistakable sense of authority, this firewall did not whisper. It roared—professionally.

3.

Hardware-wise, the PA-4020 was no slouch. Twelve Gigabit Ethernet ports (10 data, 2 HA) gave it the flexibility to segment, route, and protect multiple networks simultaneously. It also had management and console ports for out-of-band access. It's the networking equivalent of having both a combat knife and a clipboard—ready for action and documentation.

4.

It delivered up to **2 Gbps of firewall throughput, 1 Gbps of threat prevention**, and supported **250,000 max concurrent sessions**. For its time, that was spicy. Today? It still holds its own in smaller data centers or in networks that don't stream cat videos at 4K from 200 endpoints simultaneously.

5.

The operating system? PAN-OS, of course. This meant App-ID, User-ID, Content-ID, and WildFire were all included right out of the box. The same secret sauce used on the high-end PA-7000s was already bubbling away in the 4020. Same intelligence, more gristle.

6.

App-ID allowed the 4020 to surgically identify traffic by behavior, not ports. Whether it was Gmail over 443 or a sneaky gaming session cloaked in HTTPS, the 4020 called it out with zero hesitation. This box could spot an app in a snowstorm and block it before anyone noticed their fantasy football site went down.

7.

User-ID integration was equally potent. Tie user identities to policies through Active Directory, RADIUS, or even Captive Portal. The 4020 made it personal—literally. When an employee tried to VPN into a forbidden streaming site, the logs didn't just say "blocked traffic." They said "Greg. Again."

8.

Content-ID brought full-featured threat prevention, file blocking, URL filtering, and data leak protection. In-line antivirus and anti-spyware scanning meant nothing got through uninspected. It wasn't just watching traffic—it was interrogating it, scanning it, and sending it packing if it even *thought* about doing something shady.

9.

WildFire support added the final flourish. Suspicious executables, PDFs, and unknown payloads were sent to Palo Alto's global cloud sandbox. If a file misbehaved, WildFire flagged it and told every other WildFire-enabled firewall about it. The 4020 wasn't just learning—it was teaching, too.

10.

Deployment flexibility was excellent. Virtual wire mode? Check. Layer 2? Layer 3? Absolutely. Whether it needed to route, bridge, or transparently monitor, the PA-4020 slipped into your architecture like a custom-fitted glove with a sniffer and a badge.

11.

It came with full support for routing protocols: OSPF, BGP, RIP, static routes, and policy-based routing. Yes, RIP still existed when this was released. And yes, it supported it. Sometimes you just have to secure a legacy network with legacy tools—and the 4020 didn't judge.

12.

High Availability was a cornerstone feature. The PA-4020 supported active/passive HA configurations that allowed seamless failover between units. If one unit crashed, rebooted, or was "accidentally" unplugged by a clumsy intern, the other took over instantly—like a firewall ninja in waiting.

13.

On the management side, you got the holy trinity: Web GUI, CLI via SSH/console, and Panorama support. You could configure it with clicks, command lines, or centralized policy templates. If flexibility had a firewall avatar, it would wear the 4020 badge with pride.

14.

Logging and reporting were enterprise-grade. Real-time monitoring, detailed session logs, threat reports, and customizable dashboards gave admins all the visibility they could handle. Pair it with Panorama, and you were practically omniscient.

15.

SSL decryption was supported, though with the hardware of the era, it required careful planning. You could decrypt HTTPS, but don't go asking it to handle 500 encrypted YouTube streams without a little sweat. Prioritize and optimize—and the 4020 would work wonders.

16.

It also offered GlobalProtect VPN capabilities. Employees could connect securely from anywhere, and administrators could enforce endpoint posture checks, multi-factor authentication, and policy enforcement. It was a mobile security perimeter in a surprisingly polite form factor.

17.

You got the full suite of Palo Alto subscriptions: Threat Prevention, URL Filtering, GlobalProtect, WildFire, and Support. Licenses were modular, letting you choose your level of paranoia. (We recommend "high." It's the default setting for firewalls and coffee-fueled sysadmins.)

18.

Fans? Yes—plural. And they made their presence known. Not "jet engine" loud, but certainly not quiet. The 4020 came with redundant, hot-swappable fans and a noticeable hum—kind of like a diesel truck idling outside your data center, but with fewer emissions and more intrusion prevention.

19.

Power draw ranged between 200–250 watts depending on workload. It wasn't dainty, but it wasn't outrageous either. The 4020 was built to run 24/7 without complaint, just so long as you fed it enough airflow and a clean UPS.

20.

Captive portal was customizable and effective. You could redirect unauthenticated users to a login page, drop in your logo, and deliver security policy with just enough snark to make it memorable. Bonus points if you used Comic Sans.

21.

Role-based access control was another key feature. You could assign different access levels to admins, auditors, and part-time IT interns who just wanted to look at logs and feel important. The PA-4020 enforced policy even on its own users—because trust is earned, not assumed.

22.

Yes, it's end-of-sale now. But in its prime, the PA-4020 was the backbone of many mid-size and large enterprises. You can still find these loyal workhorses powering branch sites, school districts, and that one manufacturing plant that refuses to update anything unless it physically catches fire.

23.

Performance-wise, it's no match for today's 10G monsters, but it still handles SMB traffic with class. If your use case involves consistent 1Gbps or less, and you're okay with not decrypting every packet on Earth, the 4020 still has life in it.

24.

For many admins, the PA-4020 was their first "real" enterprise firewall. It was where they cut their teeth, built their first Panorama deployments, and experienced the magic of application-based security. It taught a generation of network defenders to think beyond ports and protocols.

25.

In the grand family of Palo Alto Networks firewalls, the PA-4020 is the responsible older cousin who bought a house, paid off their car, and still runs a marathon every April. It wasn't flashy. It wasn't noisy (well, except the fans). But it was powerful, trustworthy, and ready to take your enterprise into the next era of network security. Long live the gateway.

Chapter 6: PA-4050 – Now We're Talking (Loud Fans Included)

1.

The PA-4050 didn't come to *join* the network—it came to *run* it. If the PA-4020 was the diplomatic enterprise firebox, the 4050 was the one that brought a megaphone, some combat boots, and a checklist titled "Things to Secure Today." It had more ports, more power, and yes— more fan noise. This was Palo Alto showing it wasn't just playing in the enterprise pool. It was cannonballing into it.

2.

At a glance, the PA-4050 looked nearly identical to its 4020 sibling—same 2U rack-mounted chassis, same cool aluminum aesthetic, same management layout. But the hardware inside wasn't just a bump; it was a leap. If the 4020 was a tactician, the 4050 was the battle-hardened sergeant shouting "MOVE!" to packets.

3.

Equipped with 12 Gigabit Ethernet interfaces (10 for data, 2 for HA), the 4050 was made for environments with multiple zones, VLANs, DMZs, and a whole bunch of headaches waiting to be tamed. It had a dedicated management port, a console port, and a general demeanor that said, "I will route, inspect, and interrogate everything that moves."

4.

Performance took a serious jump: **up to 5 Gbps firewall throughput**, **2 Gbps threat prevention**, and **500,000 max concurrent sessions**. This made it ideal for large campuses, regional hubs, or data centers where traffic volume starts to get interesting. It was the firewall equivalent of getting promoted to enterprise overlord.

5.

PAN-OS ran at full tilt on the 4050, no compromises. You got App-ID, User-ID, Content-ID, WildFire, and the full suite of Palo Alto's best security features. This firewall didn't babysit packets—it ran background checks, DNA tests, and social media scans (figuratively… for now).

6.

App-ID was sharper than ever, identifying applications by traffic patterns instead of blind port assumptions. The 4050 could sniff out Facebook disguised as HTTPS and slap it with a deny policy before you could say "non-productive bandwidth consumption." It's the digital sniffer dog you always wanted, minus the drool.

7.

User-ID brought visibility into *who* was generating traffic, not just *what*. By syncing with Active Directory, RADIUS, or LDAP, it could tell you that Carol from Finance was uploading terabytes of spreadsheets to Dropbox. Because apparently, Q4 is serious business.

8.

Content-ID brought the hammer. Inline antivirus scanning, data leak prevention, spyware detection, URL filtering, and file-type controls all ran like a well-oiled machine. The 4050 didn't just block threats—it embarrassed them publicly and documented their entire failed attempt.

9.

And yes, WildFire support came standard. The PA-4050 could submit suspicious files to Palo Alto's cloud sandbox for detonation and analysis. It wasn't just stopping malware—it was helping the global community hunt it down and blacklist it faster than you could update your resume.

10.

Deployment flexibility included Layer 2, Layer 3, and virtual wire modes, making it a versatile fit in virtually any architecture. Whether you were dropping it in the middle of a hybrid jungle or doing a phased migration from a legacy firewall, the 4050 adapted with style—and just a bit of attitude.

11.

Routing support was extensive, with OSPF, BGP, RIP, and static routes all part of the deal. You could do policy-based routing, NAT, and even asymmetric traffic handling without the thing breaking a sweat. It was like hiring a seasoned network engineer who didn't need coffee breaks.

12.

High Availability was a given—active/passive mode ensured business continuity even if one unit took a dive. Whether it failed from hardware issues, bad firmware, or an accidental unplugging by Todd during "cable cleanup day," the secondary would pick up the slack without even flinching.

13.

Remote access? The PA-4050 had it covered. With IPsec VPN and GlobalProtect, your mobile workforce could tunnel in securely, even from that coffee shop with three Wi-Fi names and a router taped to a chair. Endpoint checks and policy enforcement made sure only clean, trusted devices got past the gate.

14.

The web-based GUI was clear, responsive, and feature-rich. CLI warriors weren't left out either —SSH and console access were as robust as ever. The 4050 respected both clickers and typists equally. It was the Switzerland of admin interfaces.

15.

Panorama integration turned the 4050 into a policy-following soldier in a centralized command structure. You could push updates, review logs, and manage multiple units across continents from a single screen. For large environments, this was an absolute game changer.

16.

Logging? Meticulous. Detailed. Obsessive. The PA-4050 tracked everything with the dedication of a private investigator and the precision of a Swiss watch. If something happened, there was a timestamped record of it—and probably a diagram, too.

17.

SSL decryption was available, and thanks to its stronger hardware, the 4050 handled it better than its younger cousins. It could inspect HTTPS traffic at scale, though careful planning was still required. As always: pick your targets, define your rules, and make sure you're not nuking performance in pursuit of perfect visibility.

18.

Fan noise? Oh yeah—it's in the name of the chapter for a reason. The PA-4050 came with powerful, front-facing, hot-swappable fans that loved to announce their presence. Put this one in a server room, not your office, unless you enjoy the ambiance of a small wind tunnel.

19.

Power consumption ranged from 250 to 300 watts. It was hungry, yes, but it was doing a lot. You fed it a clean power source, gave it room to breathe, and it returned the favor with airtight security and zero sass.

20.

It also supported captive portal features for authentication, guest access, and policy enforcement. Whether you were onboarding new users, offering restricted access to visitors, or making contractors sign a usage agreement in Comic Sans, the PA-4050 could facilitate it.

21.

Role-based administration was rock-solid. You could grant tiered access to your team, making sure junior admins couldn't accidentally wipe out rules while senior engineers maintained full control. The 4050 enforced command hierarchy better than some office managers.

22.

Subscription services included all the usual heavy-hitters: Threat Prevention, WildFire, URL Filtering, and GlobalProtect. Each license added real functionality and wasn't just a box-ticking exercise. This firewall earned its keep—every penny.

23.

Even though the PA-4050 is now end-of-sale, you can still find it dutifully humming away in older data centers, school districts, and companies where "If it works, don't replace it" is the sacred law. And honestly? It still performs like a champ—just maybe not at 2025 cloud-scale.

24.

This model bridged the gap between entry-level enterprise and true high-performance security. For many admins, it was the first time they saw what next-gen firewalling *really* looked like— full visibility, fine-grained control, and a command center that didn't make you want to cry.

25.

The PA-4050 was the loud, proud, enterprise-ready firewall that told the world, "We're not a startup anymore." With serious throughput, deep inspection, and fans that could double as a leaf blower, it was a statement piece for any rack. And while it may have aged out of the spotlight, it carved its name into enterprise history with grit, grace, and a whole lot of airflow.

Chapter 7: PA-4060 – The Refined Dinosaur

1.

The PA-4060 wasn't here to play—it was here to outlive your storage cabinets, outsmart your routers, and outfan *everything*. Nicknamed affectionately (and sometimes resentfully) in IT circles as "The Dinosaur," this enterprise heavyweight had refined taste, raw power, and a shelf life longer than some security teams' turnover cycles.

2.

Physically, the PA-4060 looked like a beast that had opinions about your cabling. With its 2U rackmount chassis, reinforced metallic body, and fans that sounded like they were prepping for takeoff, it wasn't subtle. This firewall didn't purr—it *growled*, politely.

3.

It came with 16 Gigabit Ethernet ports—plenty of room for large-scale segmentation, high-availability configurations, and even redundant ISPs or parallel DMZs. You also got your standard management and console ports, plus dual power supplies for redundancy because enterprise networks don't sleep, and neither should their firewalls.

4.

Throughput was a major step up from its 4050 sibling: **10 Gbps firewall performance**, **4 Gbps of threat prevention**, and **1 million concurrent sessions**. This thing didn't blink at 10,000 employees or multiple campuses. It greeted peak traffic like an old friend and asked if it brought snacks.

5.

PAN-OS was fully loaded, as expected. App-ID, User-ID, Content-ID, and WildFire came baked in. While the 4060 might've been released years ago, it always stayed up to date in the feature department—refined, polished, and never left behind at the protocol party.

6.

App-ID continued to be the traffic whisperer. It didn't just guess at applications—it *knew* them. Whether someone was trying to sneak Spotify through port 443 or stream high-definition Twitch under the radar, the 4060 caught it, named it, and put it in a security policy timeout.

7.

User-ID made visibility more than just IPs—it added names, roles, and sometimes judgmental sighs. By tying user activity to identities from Active Directory, LDAP, or RADIUS, the PA-4060 let you know it wasn't just "someone" uploading 3GB to Dropbox—it was *Alan*. Again.

8.

Content-ID was sharper than ever, filtering out malware, spyware, and data leaks with laser precision. It blocked bad URLs, enforced corporate compliance, and made sure nobody emailed the employee handbook to an anonymous ProtonMail address.

9.

WildFire integration meant zero-day threats had a nemesis. Unknown files were shipped off to Palo Alto's cloud sandbox, detonated in a safe virtual environment, and then classified for your firewall and every other firewall in the networked universe. Collective intelligence, Jurassic edition.

10.

Deployment options were flexible, with full support for Layer 2, Layer 3, and virtual wire modes. You could slot it into existing topologies or design around it like a paranoid architect— either way, the 4060 played nicely... unless something was malicious, in which case, no mercy.

11.

Routing? Like a champ. OSPF, BGP, RIP, and static options were all supported. It handled NAT with elegance, policy-based routing with ease, and asymmetric traffic like it was born for chaos. This dinosaur could do calculus while balancing a DNS server on its head.

12.

High Availability wasn't a feature—it was a lifestyle. The PA-4060 handled active/passive failover with grace and speed, ensuring minimal disruption even when chaos struck. If one unit dropped dead, the backup picked up the baton mid-stride. Think of it as Jurassic redundancy.

13.

GlobalProtect integration was native and powerful. Remote users could connect securely from anywhere—beach, hotel, satellite office, alien mothership. The PA-4060 didn't care. It just checked endpoint posture and made sure the device wasn't bringing malware to the party.

14.

The web GUI was robust and enterprise-ready, but the real heroes knew the CLI. SSH into this unit, and you were talking directly to a hardened beast of a security platform. Whether you preferred GUI clicking or CLI slicing, the 4060 let you configure, analyze, and control with finesse.

15.

Panorama support was superb. Centralized management made scaling policies across multiple firewalls easy. Log collection, global policy enforcement, and real-time event correlation became possible—even pleasant—with this behemoth in the mix.

16.

Logging was, of course, meticulous. Every session, threat, and alert was timestamped, indexed, and logged like it was going in front of a judge. Whether for audits, incident response, or your quarterly "What Just Happened?" report, the 4060 kept receipts.

17.

SSL decryption was available, but—like any refined dinosaur—it preferred moderation. It could handle moderate volumes of encrypted inspection, but asking it to decrypt the entire corporate Netflix habit? Not recommended. Be selective, and it'll work wonders.

18.

The PA-4060 had multiple fans, each louder than the last. And while they did a stellar job keeping the hardware cool, they also made sure you *knew* they were doing a stellar job. If quiet is your thing, install this firewall far, far away from your desk. Like, two buildings over.

19.

Power draw wasn't exactly green. It pulled around 350 watts on average—less than a server, more than a toaster, and far louder than both combined. But every watt went toward one thing: securing everything it could see with extreme prejudice.

20.

You also had captive portal options for guest access, user authentication, and temporary policy assignments. Customize your login page, slap on your company logo, and throw in some passive-aggressive login reminders. The PA-4060 supports your branding ambitions *and* your security goals.

21.

Admin roles were fully granular. You could restrict access per feature, limit visibility, or delegate specific functions. No more junior admins deleting policies "to test something." The 4060 said, "You can look—but don't touch unless I say so."

22.

Subscription licensing was required for some advanced features, but every one was worth it. Threat Prevention brought real-time security. WildFire enabled malware preemption. URL Filtering kept web traffic in line. GlobalProtect gave you secure remote access. Each license was a superpower add-on for your dino.

23.

Yes, the PA-4060 is end-of-life now, but don't assume that means obsolete. Many are still live in hardened environments, running smoothly, patched up, and holding the line like ancient guardians of the digital realm. Long may they roar.

24.

This firewall marked a turning point in enterprise-grade inspection. It was the first "big box" that many network teams deployed and realized, "Hey, this thing is *seriously* good." It wasn't cheap. It wasn't quiet. But it was one of the best security investments of its time.

25.

The PA-4060 was a refined dinosaur—built with muscle, brains, and absolutely no tolerance for threats. It gave enterprises their first taste of serious next-gen firewalling at scale, and it set the tone for everything that followed. And while it may rumble like a T-Rex on Red Bull, it earned its place in firewall history with dignity, uptime, and unmatched beeping authority.

Chapter 8: PA-5020 – Data Center Entry Level

1.

Enter the **PA-5020**, the firewall equivalent of a freshly promoted enterprise lieutenant. Built to stand guard at the edge of your data center or lead security for your core infrastructure, the 5020 wasn't just another box with ports—it was the Palo Alto that said, "Let's get serious. But not *too* serious." You know, entry-level data center seriousness.

2.

Housed in a 2U rackmount form, the PA-5020 looks unassuming, but inside? Oh, it's pure business. Think of it as the networking world's quiet professional—it won't brag, but it can block botnets, decrypt SSL, and forward logs faster than your interns can say "Oops."

3.

You got **16 Gigabit Ethernet ports**—twelve for data, two for HA, one for management, and one for console. Perfect for a data center that's just grown out of its "we used to be a startup" phase. That port count? Chef's kiss for zone segmentation, ISP redundancy, and DMZ juggling.

4.

Now let's talk performance. With **5 Gbps of firewall throughput, 2 Gbps of threat prevention**, and **1 million sessions supported**, the PA-5020 had more than enough gas to fuel medium-sized enterprises and moderate traffic-happy data centers. It didn't need to flex—numbers spoke for it.

5.

The PA-5020 ran full **PAN-OS**, which meant App-ID, User-ID, Content-ID, and WildFire were all ready to roll. None of this "lite" version nonsense. This box was a full-blown Palo Alto Networks firewall with all the good stuff, no shortcuts.

6.

App-ID on the 5020 was like a traffic-savvy detective with X-ray glasses. It knew what apps were being used, no matter how they tried to hide. Whether it was DNS tunneling or chat apps masquerading as HTTPS, the 5020 called them out and blocked them like an overprotective bouncer at Club Bandwidth.

7.

User-ID integration gave policies teeth. It wasn't just "block IP X"—it was "why is Karen from HR uploading a 4GB zip file to an unknown server?" By tying traffic to users, departments, and roles, you could enforce policies with the nuance of an HR manager and the resolve of a firewall.

8.

Content-ID was the muscle behind the brain. With deep packet inspection, threat detection, and file blocking, it did more than filter URLs—it evaluated intent. If malware tried sneaking in, Content-ID stopped it with the grace of a ballet dancer and the precision of a laser-guided missile.

9.

WildFire integration allowed the 5020 to sandbox suspicious files in the cloud. Executables, PDFs, Office files—if they looked shady, they got shipped out, detonated, analyzed, and judged. All in real-time, and all with the confidence of a cloud-powered security oracle.

10.

Routing protocols? All present and accounted for: OSPF, BGP, RIP, static, and policy-based. Whether you were at the network edge, in a multi-site mesh, or migrating from legacy gear, the 5020 could route traffic smarter than your Layer 3 switch and with a much better sense of self-worth.

11.

Deployment options were robust. Layer 3 for routing, Layer 2 for switching, and virtual wire for transparent drop-ins. Want to replace a legacy firewall mid-stream without rearchitecting everything? The PA-5020 politely said, "Allow me."

12.

High Availability came in active/passive flavors. Two units could sync and failover seamlessly, ensuring that your boss would never notice a thing went wrong—unless he saw the alerts you emailed *after* the failover worked flawlessly.

13.

GlobalProtect support was built in, giving remote employees secure access without putting your infrastructure at risk. Whether they were on a train, in a coffee shop, or "working remotely" from a beach, the 5020 ensured encrypted, policy-enforced sessions with full visibility.

14.

The GUI interface? Top-notch. PAN-OS offered clean menus, intuitive dashboards, and just the right number of graphs to make middle management feel like they understood security. Meanwhile, CLI fans could dive deep via SSH, whipping up routing tables and traffic captures like it was a gourmet hobby.

15.

Panorama integration made managing multiple PA-5020s a breeze. Push policies, collect logs, monitor traffic, and control it all from one place. Think of it like a control tower for your entire Palo Alto fleet—with none of the screaming into headsets.

16.

Logging and reporting were enterprise-caliber. You got real-time threat alerts, session logs, and customizable reporting to make audits less of a week-long panic session. If something got through, you'd know when, where, how, and whether Dave in QA clicked it.

17.

SSL decryption was fully supported. This box could inspect encrypted traffic with confidence, as long as you respected its resource limits. It was like giving a guard dog X-ray vision—as long as you didn't expect it to see through *everything* at once.

18.

The fans, of course, were back. Not jet-engine loud, but certainly present. They worked hard to keep the internals chilled and often made themselves known like a polite background hum that whispered, "I'm protecting you from ransomware right now."

19.

Power draw was about **350 to 400 watts**, depending on configuration. That's not light, but it's not outrageous either for what this thing delivered. Just don't plug it into the same UPS as the snack machine or chaos may ensue.

20.

Captive portal functionality gave you the option to force user logins for guest networks, BYOD zones, or that one weird warehouse with 12 unmanaged barcode scanners. Customize the splash page, slap on your logo, and enforce identity—no anonymous browsing here.

21.

Role-based access meant you could give the intern just enough access to check logs, but not enough to *accidentally* delete half the security policies. Granular control isn't just good hygiene —it's essential in enterprise networks where "Oops" can cost millions.

22.

Licensing followed the standard Palo Alto model: pick your subscriptions (Threat Prevention, WildFire, GlobalProtect, URL Filtering), and let the firewall level up like it just cleared a security dungeon. Each license added visibility, protection, and bragging rights.

23.
Though the PA-5020 is end-of-life today, it remains one of the most beloved Palo Alto models ever deployed. Reliable, consistent, and smart—it was like the Toyota Camry of firewalls. Not flashy, but so well-built it kept going far longer than anyone expected.

24.
For many teams, the 5020 was their first foray into serious data center firewalling. It handled real workloads, massive logs, encrypted traffic, and VPNs all in one sleek unit. It was your first taste of enterprise protection—without a six-figure budget or a team of ten.

25.
The PA-5020 was the perfect gateway to real enterprise firepower. It offered smart, scalable protection with next-gen features in a package that balanced capability and cost. Loud enough to be heard, powerful enough to be trusted, and reliable enough to be remembered—it was the firewall you needed before you even knew how badly you needed it.

Chapter 9: PA-5050 – Speed and Signatures, Together at Last

1.
The **PA-5050** didn't arrive quietly—it entered the data center like a boss with a badge, a clipboard, and a full threat signature database. Designed for high-speed environments that needed serious inspection horsepower, it was Palo Alto's answer to, "Can we go faster *and* be more secure?" Spoiler alert: Yes. Yes, you can.

2.
From the outside, the PA-5050 looked like its 5020 sibling on a high-protein diet—same 2U rackmount size, but with guts upgraded to handle the traffic flow of demanding enterprise and service provider environments. It wasn't just the next model up. It was a declaration.

3.
The PA-5050 featured **20 Gigabit Ethernet ports** (16 data, 2 HA, 1 management, 1 console), plus **dual power supplies** for redundancy. That's more ports than a modest-sized switch. If your network topology looked like a spiderweb with ambitions, the 5050 was your hub.

4.
Let's get into numbers. **20 Gbps firewall throughput**, **10 Gbps threat prevention**, and support for **2 million concurrent sessions** made this unit a juggernaut in its class. That's not entry-level. That's "hold my packet capture" territory.

5.
Of course, it ran **PAN-OS**—fully featured, no compromises. You got App-ID, User-ID, Content-ID, and WildFire baked in like a four-layer security lasagna. Everything Palo Alto had to offer, this unit could handle—and at speed.

6.

App-ID on the 5050 was terrifyingly effective. It didn't just inspect traffic; it interrogated it. Whether apps were hiding behind common ports or wrapped in encrypted tunnels, the 5050 peeled them open and identified them like an overzealous customs agent.

7.

User-ID turned IP addresses into actual human accountability. It tied traffic to Active Directory users, local accounts, or third-party identity sources. When someone violated policy, the 5050 could tell you exactly *who* did it—no more "it was the guest Wi-Fi" excuses.

8.

Content-ID performed DPI with elegance and aggression. Viruses, malware, exploit kits, and even mildly suspicious PDFs were scanned, flagged, and blocked. It also filtered URLs, inspected SSL (when configured), and ensured corporate data didn't wander into the wild.

9.

WildFire? Fully integrated. Unknown files were shipped off to the global sandbox for detonation, classification, and signature generation. Within minutes, your PA-5050 and every other Palo Alto firewall in the universe knew about the latest threat. Welcome to community-powered defense.

10.

The **PA-5050** was built for **large campuses, high-speed enterprise cores**, and **data centers with trust issues**. If your network pumped out gigabits like it was going out of style, the 5050 filtered, analyzed, and logged it without so much as a hiccup.

11.

Deployment modes included Layer 3, Layer 2, and virtual wire. Whether you were replacing an aging perimeter box, doing a stealth bump-in-the-wire for threat inspection, or building the Fort Knox of hybrid networks, the 5050 fit like a tailored blazer—with armor.

12.

Routing support was as expected: BGP, OSPF, RIP, static, and PBR. With advanced NAT and QoS, this box was ready for any traffic scenario you threw at it. Dual-ISP routing? Done. Complex internal segmentation with NAT exemptions? Child's play.

13.

High Availability came standard, and the failover was slick. You could pair two 5050s in active/passive mode, complete with full session sync and health monitoring. When one fell, the other stood taller. It was firewall loyalty, codified.

14.

The GUI was classic PAN-OS: visual, snappy, and designed for both security pros and accidental-clickers. CLI access was equally powerful, allowing for deep diagnostics, scripting, and live packet captures—all from your favorite SSH terminal.

15.

Panorama integration made managing fleets of 5050s across multiple data centers not just possible, but efficient. Global rule push, central log aggregation, and real-time health monitoring —all the nerdy, beautiful things security architects dream about.

16.

The logging engine was relentless. Threat logs, traffic logs, system alerts, configuration changes —it documented everything. If a packet sneezed on its way through, the 5050 logged it, timestamped it, and probably suggested a tissue.

17.

SSL decryption was robust, but—as with all firewalls—required strategic application. You could decrypt traffic from finance apps, suspicious categories, or anything not nailed down. Just be mindful of CPU load, and don't try to decrypt *all of YouTube* on a Friday afternoon.

18.

With fans that meant business and a hum that could lull network engineers into a deep, packet-inspection trance, the 5050 wasn't whisper-quiet. But it was tolerable—and in many data centers, a background symphony of reliability.

19.

Power draw ranged from **400 to 500 watts**, depending on throughput and traffic profile. That's decent for a firewall juggling millions of sessions and deep-inspecting 10 Gbps of malware-laced chaos. Just make sure your PDU isn't shared with the snack fridge.

20.

GlobalProtect VPN services were fully supported, enabling remote workers to securely access the corporate network with policy enforcement. Whether connecting from home, a café, or their in-laws' basement, users got secure tunnels and consistent security enforcement.

21.

Role-based administration was strong. Give read-only access to the compliance auditor, full access to your lead engineer, and CLI-only access to the overly enthusiastic intern. Everyone gets just enough power to be useful—not dangerous.

22.

Captive portal options allowed for guest access, BYOD onboarding, and internal user authentication with custom splash pages. Want to throw in your company logo, a usage policy, or a dad joke? The PA-5050 supports all three.

23.

Licensing was modular, as always. You activated Threat Prevention, URL Filtering, GlobalProtect, and WildFire features a la carte—or went all-in. Each license added layers of security that made the 5050 an even more fearsome gatekeeper.

24.

Even as newer models outpaced it, the PA-5050 remains a legend in enterprise networks. It was reliable, powerful, and efficient—a trifecta in the security world. Many are still humming along in secondary data centers, test labs, or tucked behind dusty cables doing what they do best: protecting.

25.

The PA-5050 was Palo Alto's first truly high-speed, threat-prevention juggernaut. It blended throughput with deep inspection and helped organizations transition from perimeter filtering to full-spectrum, application-aware security. Speed and signatures weren't mutually exclusive

Chapter 10: PA-5060 – The OG Titan

If the PA-5020 was the gateway and the PA-5050 was the enforcer, then the PA-5060 was the undisputed Titan of Palo Alto's first-gen heavyweights. Built for scale, stress, and security that didn't blink, this firewall stomped into data centers and said, "Try me."

The 5060 wasn't sleek—it was solid. With a 2U chassis that looked like it could survive a fall down a stairwell (don't try that), this unit demanded respect. Its rack presence said one thing loud and clear: "I am not here to be quiet, and I am not here to fail."

You got 20 Gigabit Ethernet ports, full front-panel visibility, and two hot-swappable fans that doubled as your data center's unofficial white noise machine. Also included: dual power supplies, just in case one decided to pull a mid-shift nap. Redundancy? Absolutely.

Under the hood, the PA-5060 delivered up to 20 Gbps of firewall throughput, 10 Gbps of threat prevention, and 4 million concurrent sessions. That's not just enterprise-level—that's enterprise-with-a-data-lake-and-global-offices level.

Running full PAN-OS, the 5060 included all the goodies: App-ID, User-ID, Content-ID, and WildFire support. It didn't come to pick and choose—it came to inspect every byte, flag every threat, and log every questionable decision made by Kevin in DevOps.

App-ID let this beast track and control applications with uncanny precision. Facebook chat hiding inside HTTPS? Caught. Remote desktop on a weird port? Flagged. BitTorrent posing as DNS? Shut. Down. The 5060 could detect app-level threats without needing a Ouija board or guesswork.

User-ID made policy personal. It didn't just see an IP address—it saw Jane from Finance using an out-of-date browser to access an unsanctioned cloud app. And with that knowledge came precise policy enforcement. Sorry, Jane.

Content-ID brought the deep-packet hammer. With built-in antivirus, anti-spyware, and vulnerability protection, the 5060 didn't filter traffic—it cross-examined it, scanned it, and only allowed passage if it passed the vibe check (and the threat signatures).

WildFire rounded out the suite, allowing unknown files to be sent to Palo Alto's sandbox for detonation and classification. New threats? No problem. Once one 5060 spotted it, the rest of the fleet around the world updated in minutes. Think Skynet, but on your side.

Deployment modes? Yes, all of them. Whether Layer 2, Layer 3, or virtual wire, the PA-5060 fit into your design like a perfectly coded function—clean, efficient, and ready to throw punches at packet-level shenanigans.

Routing was robust: OSPF, BGP, RIP, static routes, policy-based forwarding. Whether your network looked like a tiered enterprise architecture or a spaghetti diagram drawn in panic at 2AM, the 5060 could route it, NAT it, and secure it—all at once.

High Availability was as expected—top tier. The 5060 paired with another 5060 like a firewall soulmate. Active/passive with full state sync meant that if one went belly-up, the other sprang into action with barely a dropped packet. It's not failover; it's flawless-over.

GlobalProtect VPN was built-in, allowing secure access from anywhere on the globe. Whether your users were remote, hybrid, or working from a van parked near a coffee shop with "borrowed" Wi-Fi, the 5060 gave them secure tunnels with policy enforcement.

The GUI was the same reliable PAN-OS dashboard, with charts, logs, and dashboards that made even the most cynical auditor nod in approval. For the command-line faithful, SSH access brought all the deep-level diagnostics you could dream of—packet captures included.

Panorama made managing multiple PA-5060s (and their smaller cousins) a centralized dream. Push policies, review logs, analyze threat trends—all from one console. The PA-5060 didn't just scale; it scaled smart.

Logging was exhaustive. Traffic logs, threat logs, config changes, system events—you could recreate a complete network crime scene with timestamped forensic detail. The 5060 didn't just remember—it archived your sins.

SSL decryption was fully supported, and the 5060 had the horsepower to handle it without wheezing. You could decrypt selectively (and wisely), inspect the payload, and apply full threat prevention—all while watching your CPU hum with confidence, not panic.

Its fans were… noticeable. Not "hairdryer" loud, but definitely not silent. They kicked in with a sense of purpose, like the firewall was warming up for a wrestling match with ransomware. If you're installing it near people, invest in earplugs or a longer cable.

Power draw landed between 450 to 550 watts, depending on usage. That's respectable for the level of protection it offered. Pro tip: make sure your rack has good airflow and maybe don't stack it under your espresso machine.

Captive portal options were onboard, letting you authenticate users in guest zones, BYOD networks, and contractor segments. Whether you wanted simple login, fancy splash screens, or the dreaded "Terms and Conditions" checkbox—this box did it.

Role-based access control was sharp and flexible. You could give your SOC team the keys to the kingdom and restrict your eager junior admin to only log viewing. No more "I thought I was in staging" mistakes wiping production rules.

Licensing was à la carte and fair: Threat Prevention, URL Filtering, GlobalProtect, WildFire, and more. Activate what you need, skip what you don't, and know that every feature is battle-tested and enterprise-grade.

Even though the PA-5060 is now officially end-of-sale, it's still out there. Hospitals, universities, government agencies, and Fortune 500s still rely on it as a secondary core firewall or high-trust zone sentry. It's not forgotten—it's legacy with loyalty.

If your first serious firewall was a PA-5060, you remember the feeling of power. It taught you about security architecture, throughput tuning, and the joy of a clean log after blocking a botnet. This wasn't just a firewall—it was a career milestone.

The PA-5060 is the OG Titan—loud, proud, powerful, and unfailingly reliable. It helped define what a next-generation firewall should be and protected thousands of networks with silent strength (and not-so-silent fans). Respect where it's due: this beast walked so modern NGFWs could sprint.

—they were a match made in firewall heaven.

Chapter 11: PA-3020 – The Midrange Marvel

1.
Say hello to the **PA-3020**, the firewall that lived in the sweet spot between "too small for real enterprise" and "overkill for branch offices." It was the Goldilocks zone of Palo Alto Networks —just enough power, just enough ports, and just enough "Wow, this thing can *really* inspect traffic."

2.
With its sleek 1U form factor, the 3020 was a welcome sight in any rack. Compact? Yes. Underpowered? Absolutely not. It was the firebox equivalent of a high-efficiency hybrid car— quietly dependable with unexpected power under the hood.

3.
The hardware layout was clean and efficient: **8 Gigabit data ports, 1 management port, 1 console**, and **2 HA ports**. It had everything you needed to segment a mid-sized network without making the rack look like a spaghetti accident.

4.
Performance was sharp: **1 Gbps firewall throughput, 500 Mbps threat prevention**, and **64,000 concurrent sessions**. That made it perfect for branch offices, educational institutions, or even corporate HQs with a sane internet plan and a decent security posture.

5.
Of course, it ran full **PAN-OS**—no shortcuts, no "lite" builds. You got all the bells and whistles: **App-ID, User-ID, Content-ID, WildFire**, and a GUI that looked like it graduated summa cum laude in UI/UX design.

6.

App-ID brought the magic. Instead of blindly allowing ports, the 3020 knew exactly what apps were doing. Whether it was Slack over TCP/443 or a suspicious browser plugin misbehaving, this firewall called it out like a coach yelling at a lazy linebacker.

7.

User-ID meant the 3020 could track traffic by *people*, not just devices. It integrated smoothly with Active Directory and RADIUS, giving you real-time identity awareness. When things went sideways, the logs didn't say "192.168.1.42"—they said "Steve did it."

8.

Content-ID was its deep-packet surgeon. This feature filtered malware, spyware, and inappropriate content faster than HR could say "policy violation." With inline antivirus, DLP, and file-type control, the 3020 could guard against threats *and* productivity-killers.

9.

WildFire added brains to the brawn. Suspicious files were automatically sent to Palo Alto's global cloud sandbox for detonation and analysis. New malware samples were studied, cataloged, and blacklisted, keeping your network smarter than the bad guys—always.

10.

Whether you deployed it in **Layer 3**, **Layer 2**, or **virtual wire mode**, the PA-3020 adapted like a pro. It could sit silently in a network and inspect traffic transparently or act as a full-blown routing gateway with NAT and policy-based routing on the side.

11.

Routing protocols? Check. It supported **OSPF, BGP, RIP**, and **static routes**, giving you the control you needed in even the messiest network diagrams. And with full **QoS support**, the 3020 could also prioritize voice, video, or Karen's desperate need for Excel.

12.

High Availability came standard. With active/passive failover and full session syncing, you could double up your 3020s and sleep better at night. If one firewall had a bad day, the other picked up the slack like a best friend at crunch time.

13.

GlobalProtect was baked in and beautiful. Road warriors and remote workers could connect securely with endpoint health checks and identity enforcement. Your VPN didn't just tunnel—it authenticated, inspected, and enforced corporate policy.

14.

The GUI was that classic Palo Alto sweet spot—responsive, modern, and dare we say, *fun* to use. And if you preferred the command line? SSH in and flex your CLI muscles with advanced commands, real-time logging, and packet captures that made your PCAP dreams come true.

15.

Panorama integration meant managing multiple PA-3020s (or any mix of Palo Altos) was centralized and elegant. Push policies, pull logs, monitor traffic—all from one console. It was like playing firewall SimCity, but with better graphs.

16.

Logging was thorough, structured, and timestamped like it was headed for a courtroom. Security events, system logs, config changes—it captured it all. You could investigate issues, replay events, or just stare at the logs like they held the secrets of the universe.

17.

SSL decryption was supported, and the 3020 handled moderate encrypted traffic with dignity. Target your high-risk categories (file sharing, unknown apps), and this firewall would peek behind the curtain without melting down. Smart decryption = smarter security.

18.

The PA-3020 also offered **captive portal** features, allowing you to prompt unauthenticated users before granting access. Great for guest Wi-Fi, BYOD, or catching that mystery device named "John's iPhone 7" before it gets too comfortable.

19.

Role-based admin control let you set permissions down to the feature. Give junior admins log access only, let your security lead adjust policies, and lock the "delete all" button behind three keys and a blood oath. The 3020 kept the right hands on the right levers.

20.

Power draw hovered around **100–120 watts**, making it surprisingly energy-efficient for a firewall this capable. You could power two of them, your switch, and a small fridge and still have enough juice left over to charge your earbuds.

21.

And yes, **the fans were noticeable**. Not hairdryer-loud, but enough to say "Hey, I'm working here." As long as you didn't install it next to your desk, you were fine. In a rack, it was background ambiance for security peace of mind.

22.

Licensing followed the usual suspects: **Threat Prevention, URL Filtering, WildFire, and GlobalProtect** subscriptions all available à la carte. Each license added real capabilities, not just marketing fluff—and let's be real, the combo was pretty lethal (in a good way).

23.

Though the 3020 is officially **end-of-sale**, it's still active in a ton of networks—especially education, government, and mid-sized enterprise sites where reliability still beats flash. You'll find them humming happily, doing their job like seasoned pros.

24.

For many IT admins, the PA-3020 was the first "real" enterprise firewall they configured themselves. It taught them PAN-OS, application control, and why packet filtering alone was so 2005. It built confidence—and careers.

25.

The PA-3020 was a true midrange marvel: smart, steady, and fully loaded. It made next-gen security accessible, flexible, and affordable for networks that didn't need a data center-sized monster. In the Palo Alto firewall family tree, this one was the reliable middle child who showed up early, stayed late, and never asked for a raise.

Chapter 12: PA-3050 – The MVP of Mid-Sized IDS

1.

If the PA-3020 was the smart, dependable middle child, then the **PA-3050** was the older sibling who hit the gym, took night classes in cybersecurity, and still had time to pick up your packets from school. It was the midrange workhorse with enough horsepower to anchor a medium enterprise and enough finesse to impress your auditors.

2.

Designed in the same compact 1U form factor as its 3020 sibling, the PA-3050 looked innocent enough. But beneath that unassuming shell was a threat prevention machine that could handle more connections, more throughput, and—let's be honest—more nonsense from misbehaving endpoints.

3.

The PA-3050 sported **8 Gigabit Ethernet ports**, a **management port**, **console port**, and **2 HA ports**, giving you the flexibility to segment, route, and failover without breaking a sweat. It also came with a confident stance and the cool attitude of, "Yeah, I got this."

4.

Where it really shined was performance: **4 Gbps of firewall throughput, 2 Gbps of threat prevention**, and **128,000 max sessions**. That's double the 3020 in most categories, making the 3050 a favorite for headquarters, school districts, and regional offices with serious data appetites.

5.

Naturally, it ran **PAN-OS**, delivering full **App-ID, User-ID, Content-ID, and WildFire** integration. There were no shortcuts here—this was the full Palo Alto experience, compressed into a 1U rocket ship of DPI goodness.

6.

App-ID allowed you to ditch the outdated port-centric mindset. The 3050 didn't guess—it *knew* what application was talking. Whether it was Dropbox wrapped in SSL or gaming traffic sneaking through port 443, the 3050 exposed it, labeled it, and (optionally) annihilated it.

7.

With **User-ID**, the PA-3050 could tie activity to real users, not just IP addresses. It turned anonymous traffic into named accountability—"Looks like Bob in Finance just downloaded a 700MB ISO from a Romanian file server again." Thanks, Bob.

8.

Content-ID provided deep-packet inspection with enough depth to make sharks nervous. It blocked malware, filtered URLs, enforced data leak policies, and stopped everything from zero-day exploits to casual copy/paste violations of corporate secrets.

9.

And then there was **WildFire**, the threat-intelligence engine that took every sketchy file, yeeted it into a virtual sandbox, and watched it try to misbehave. If it acted up, it got flagged, classified, and blocked—not just on your 3050, but across all WildFire-enabled firewalls globally.

10.

Deployment options were, of course, flexible: **Layer 3**, **Layer 2**, and **virtual wire**. Whether you were deploying transparently, bridging VLANs, or creating a gateway choke point, the PA-3050 showed up like a bouncer with a clipboard and an advanced degree in application awareness.

11.

Routing support included **OSPF, BGP, RIP, static routes**, and **policy-based forwarding**. Whether your network looked like a carefully curated topology or something drawn during a caffeine crash, the 3050 would route it with no complaints.

12.

High Availability support was built-in and enterprise-ready. Active/passive failover with session synchronization meant that if one 3050 faceplanted (power loss, firmware crash, intern misstep), the other picked up where it left off with almost psychic precision.

13.

GlobalProtect VPN functionality allowed remote users to connect securely from anywhere. With user authentication, device health checks, and consistent policy enforcement, you weren't just tunneling traffic—you were doing it right.

14.

The **GUI** was classic Palo Alto: clean, organized, and deceptively powerful. Security pros could configure advanced features, while newer admins could find their way without an instruction manual the size of a law textbook. And for the command-line crew? **CLI via SSH or console** was always there, ready to flex.

15.

Panorama integration elevated management for multi-site deployments. Push policy to all your 3050s, roll back config changes, review logs, or deploy threat signatures globally—because why do things one-by-one when you can do them like a boss?

16.

Logging was robust, exhaustive, and maybe even a little obsessive. You got traffic logs, threat logs, URL logs, system logs, and even configuration diffs. If it happened, the PA-3050 knew about it, logged it, and filed it with a timestamp and a smirk.

17.

SSL decryption was not just supported—it was expected. With beefier hardware than its younger sibling, the 3050 handled more encrypted sessions before breaking a sweat. Use it strategically to inspect where it counts (and not on grandma's baking blog).

18.

Fans? Yes, and a little louder than the 3020. You'd definitely hear it working in a small room, but in a server rack with friends, it blended into the background symphony of hums, blinks, and the occasional existential dread.

19.

Power consumption landed around **150–180 watts**, which is still impressive for a unit that could inspect 2 Gbps of DPI-laden, signature-matching madness. Eco-friendly? Maybe not. Efficient? Absolutely.

20.

Captive portal was handy for guest Wi-Fi, BYOD, and short-term device access. Customize the login page with your logo, a welcome message, or a mildly threatening usage policy—and the 3050 made sure no one bypassed it.

21.

Role-based administration let you define exactly who could access what. Your firewall expert got god-mode; the intern got view-only logs. The PA-3050 respected hierarchy—especially when mistakes could drop your VPN mid-board meeting.

22.

Licensing followed the tried-and-true format: **Threat Prevention, URL Filtering, WildFire, and GlobalProtect** could be activated independently or bundled together for the full force of next-gen security. Each one turned the 3050 into more of a juggernaut.

23.

The PA-3050 is now **end-of-sale**, but it still lives in the real world—protecting school districts, hospitals, local governments, and enterprises that don't believe in upgrading what isn't broken. And this? It never broke a sweat.

24.

For many IT teams, the 3050 was the first firewall that felt *overqualified*. It handled high-speed traffic, logged everything, decrypted SSL, and played nice with the rest of the infrastructure. It earned its title as midrange MVP with sheer consistency.

25.

The PA-3050 wasn't flashy—it was focused. A next-gen IDS with enough performance to grow, enough features to impress, and just enough noise to let you know it was alive. It defined the mid-tier firewall for its generation and remains a legend where it still roams—quietly, capably, and always scanning.

Chapter 13: PA-3060 – IDS Meets Intelligence

1.

If the PA-3050 was the MVP of mid-sized networks, then the **PA-3060** was its smarter, faster, more data-hungry sibling. It didn't just inspect traffic—it studied it, profiled it, and made judgment calls with the finesse of a security analyst who drinks black coffee and listens to packet captures for fun.

2.

In terms of looks, the PA-3060 shared the same svelte 1U design as the 3020 and 3050, but don't let that fool you. Inside, it was a performance powerhouse with a brain to match. You didn't just deploy the 3060—you unleashed it.

3.

Let's talk interfaces: **8 Gigabit Ethernet ports, 1 management, 1 console,** and **2 HA ports**. It offered enough flexibility to support complex segmentation, failover setups, and serious Layer 3 networking—all without requiring an entire rack of blinking chaos.

4.

Performance specs? Oh, it delivered. With **4 Gbps firewall throughput, 3 Gbps threat prevention,** and **256,000 max sessions**, the PA-3060 wasn't here to handle traffic—it was here to *command* it. It was like strapping a firewall to a rocket and pointing it at your east/west traffic.

5.

Running the latest **PAN-OS**, the 3060 came loaded with **App-ID, User-ID, Content-ID, and WildFire**. No cut corners, no "limited mode." Just full-spectrum Palo Alto protection designed to block everything except productivity and your boss's favorite SaaS dashboard.

6.

App-ID turned the 3060 into a protocol psychologist. It didn't guess what app was running—it analyzed, inspected, and identified. Whether it was Gmail, Signal, or an obscure niche FTP tool that only Ted in engineering uses, the 3060 caught it with surgical accuracy.

7.

User-ID brought user identity into play, making policy enforcement a personal affair. It integrated with Active Directory, RADIUS, LDAP—you name it. The 3060 didn't just block "traffic"—it blocked *Steve's* traffic when Steve forgot that using unsanctioned file-sharing apps was frowned upon.

8.

Content-ID gave it x-ray vision. With inline antivirus, spyware detection, and vulnerability protection, this firewall didn't just secure your perimeter—it sterilized your traffic. It found threats hiding in Excel sheets, PDFs, and HTTP requests that looked a little too curious.

9.

Then there was **WildFire**, the crown jewel of proactive detection. Unknown files got sandboxed, dissected, and judged like they were trying out for a malware reality show. If they acted shady, they were flagged, and new threat intel was pushed out globally faster than your lunch break ended.

10.

Deployment options? It did **Layer 3**, **Layer 2**, and **virtual wire** like a networking ninja. Whether you dropped it transparently between two switches or set it up as your gateway, the 3060 adapted to the environment like it had studied your network map in advance.

11.

Routing support was top-tier. OSPF, BGP, RIP, static, and policy-based routing were all in its toolkit. You could run it at the core, the edge, or somewhere in between, and it would route packets with confidence and zero attitude.

12.

High Availability was fully supported, with active/passive modes and complete session synchronization. If your primary 3060 gave up the ghost, the secondary stepped in like a seasoned understudy ready to take the stage—without missing a cue.

13.

GlobalProtect VPN support gave remote workers secure, policy-enforced tunnels. Whether users were on a plane, in a hotel, or hacking together a presentation at 3AM from their kitchen, the 3060 kept their sessions clean, encrypted, and protected from sketchy Wi-Fi.

14.

The **GUI** was everything you've come to expect from Palo Alto—clean, customizable, and way less scary than most "enterprise" firewalls. And for the CLI lovers? SSH access delivered full control, real-time debugging, and enough diagnostic commands to make your hair stand on end.

15.

Panorama support elevated it further. With centralized policy management, log aggregation, and one-pane-of-glass visibility, managing a fleet of 3060s felt less like work and more like security orchestration with a jazz soundtrack.

16.

Logging was comprehensive and beautiful. Real-time traffic flows, threat alerts, configuration changes, and URL logs were recorded, timestamped, and ready to be exported. The 3060 was like that one friend who remembers *everything*—but only uses their powers for good.

17.

SSL decryption? Absolutely. The 3060 handled encrypted traffic inspection with grace, allowing you to prioritize visibility where it mattered most. Decrypt healthcare sites? Maybe not. But unknown applications? Bring it on.

18.

Fans were louder than the 3020, but quieter than a 5060. They whispered "I'm doing something important" rather than screaming "I'm melting!" Overall, data center-friendly and office-acceptable—just not next to your desk, please.

19.
Power consumption was around **180–200 watts**, which was impressive considering its inspection capacity. It didn't need to be babied or micromanaged—just rack it, power it, and let it work its IDS/IPS magic.

20.
Captive portal features allowed for user authentication before granting access. Handy for Wi-Fi zones, short-term users, and those rogue devices that show up at 9:02 AM and try to sneak into the VLAN party without a wristband.

21.
Role-based access control was finely tuned. Admins could assign rights based on responsibility, technical expertise, or how much coffee they'd consumed. The intern got view-only. The SOC lead got the keys to the kingdom. Simple, smart, and secure.

22.
Licensing was modular and scalable. From **Threat Prevention** and **URL Filtering** to **GlobalProtect** and **WildFire**, each feature activated a new layer of capability. Buy what you need, skip what you don't, and still feel like a next-gen warrior.

23.
Though the 3060 is now **end-of-sale**, it lives on in many production environments—and for good reason. Its combination of performance, intelligence, and flexibility made it a favorite for orgs that wanted data center features without data center budget demands.

24.
The 3060 taught admins how to think beyond basic firewalls. It taught network segmentation, zero-trust policy structuring, and why DPI matters *even more* when everything is encrypted. It was part tool, part teacher.

25.
In the long legacy of Palo Alto firewalls, the **PA-3060** stands out as the one that blended IDS/IPS capability with intelligent, contextual inspection—without needing an entire SOC to manage it. It was small enough to fit in tight spaces, smart enough to inspect what mattered, and fast enough to earn the respect of everyone who powered it on.

Chapter 14: PA-7080 – The First Behemoth

1.
If Palo Alto firewalls had a family tree, the **PA-7080** would be the ancestor that rode in on a storm cloud, thundered across the data center, and took up residence in the top rack like a digital god. This wasn't just a firewall—it was a **platform**, a **framework**, and a **statement**. You didn't just deploy a 7080. You committed to a *lifestyle*.

2.

The PA-7080 wasn't a box—it was a **modular chassis**, standing tall at **12U** of pure ambition. Designed to protect *very* large networks, internet-scale ISPs, and Fortune 100 data centers, it had slots for **network cards, control planes, data planes**, and dreams. This was the firewall that made other firewalls feel insecure about their throughput.

3.

It came with **10-slot flexibility**, housing up to **10 Network Processing Cards (NPCs), two Switch Management Cards (SMCs)** for redundancy, and **two Control Cards (MMCs)** to run the whole operation. In short? It was the "some assembly required" of cyber defense—except the end result could inspect traffic like a bat at a mosquito convention.

4.

Performance was obscene—in the best way. We're talking **700 Gbps firewall throughput, 200 Gbps threat prevention**, and **hundreds of millions of concurrent sessions**. The PA-7080 could secure an entire country's worth of traffic before breakfast and still have time to optimize your DNS queries.

5.

Naturally, it ran full **PAN-OS** with the expected array of **App-ID, User-ID, Content-ID, and WildFire**. There were no "limited features" for this beast—it didn't just inspect traffic; it *commanded* it, judged it, and blocked it before you even clicked "Send."

6.

App-ID on the 7080 was borderline precognitive. It didn't just detect applications—it practically read their terms of service. Whether traffic came from legit sources, sketchy tunnels, or experimental apps in dev, the 7080 saw it, named it, and filed it under "Allow" or "Absolutely Not."

7.

User-ID worked across massive identity frameworks, tying user behavior to real humans—even across federated, multi-domain, and hybrid architectures. When *Derek from VendorCorp* tried to exfiltrate data, the 7080 said, "Nice try, Derek."

8.

Content-ID was turned up to eleven. With dozens of gigabits of throughput to play with, it scanned payloads for malware, phishing, command-and-control patterns, and all kinds of behavioral anomalies. Think antivirus, URL filtering, DLP, and deep-packet forensics—all running simultaneously, all smiling.

9.

WildFire support was built in and amplified. This wasn't just one box sending samples—it was a global fortress acting as both participant and sentinel. Files were detonated, analyzed, and the resulting threat intel distributed across fleets of Palo Alto units faster than your bandwidth alert could finish loading.

10.

Deployments were architectural feats: **Layer 2**, **Layer 3**, **virtual wire**, or **hybridized setups** with policy zones that spanned entire continents. If your network map required its own legend and compass, the 7080 said, "Cool. Let's do this."

11.

You had full **routing support** (OSPF, BGP, RIP, PBF, and static) and an enterprise's worth of **QoS**, **NAT**, and **security zones** to slice and dice your traffic any way you wanted. This wasn't just a firewall—it was a policy-driven war machine.

12.

The 7080 supported full **High Availability**, of course—but it also *demanded* it. Dual control planes, redundant power, cooling fans that sounded like jet engines during takeoff—everything screamed resilience. When your SLA says "five nines," the 7080 replies with a nod and a low growl.

13.

Yes, it's loud. Yes, it's power-hungry. And yes, it deserves its own power feed and cooling strategy. But if your data center needs to scale securely at ridiculous speeds, this was—and in many places still *is*—the gold standard of IDS/IPS hardware firewalls.

14.

The PA-7080 wasn't just Palo Alto's first behemoth—it was a shift in mindset. It proved that deep inspection and scalable throughput could coexist, and it laid the groundwork for a future where firewalls didn't just keep up with traffic—they owned it. This isn't just legacy. This is **legend**.

Chapter 15: PA-220 – Cute, Quiet, and Competent

1.

If the PA-7080 was a warship, then the **PA-220** is a stealth kayak—silent, sleek, and surprisingly dangerous for its size. This little firewall didn't need fanfare. It needed a desk, an internet connection, and the opportunity to prove that good things come in tiny, passively cooled packages.

2.

The PA-220 is a **desktop-class next-gen firewall**, designed for **small offices, branch deployments, retail stores**, and even **home labs with ambition issues**. It's the kind of box that quietly protects your entire environment while occupying less space than a paperback.

3.

At just over 1 pound, with **8 Gigabit Ethernet ports**, a **USB console port**, and one **dedicated management port**, the PA-220 somehow fits full PAN-OS functionality into something that looks like it could run a smart toaster. But don't let its size fool you—this thing inspects.

4.

Performance-wise, it delivers **500 Mbps firewall throughput**, **150 Mbps of threat prevention**, and **64,000 concurrent sessions**. That's more than enough for **20–50 users**, especially when you want next-gen features without next-gen power bills.

5.

And yes—it runs **full PAN-OS**, just like its beefier siblings. **App-ID, User-ID, Content-ID, WildFire**, and **GlobalProtect** are all available. It's not a toy—it's just humble.

6.

App-ID lets the PA-220 detect and control apps by behavior and signature, not just ports. Want to allow Google Drive but block YouTube? Easy. Want to throttle Skype but allow Teams? Done. This little box reads traffic like a seasoned bouncer reads fake IDs.

7.

User-ID allows you to tie policies to real humans via Active Directory, LDAP, or RADIUS. Instead of "192.168.1.18 tried to access forbiddencontent.com," you'll see "Kyle in Accounting." And Kyle will have some explaining to do.

8.

Content-ID is where the PA-220 earns its keep. Antivirus, anti-spyware, file-type control, URL filtering—it's all here. It'll inspect web traffic, block malware, and keep users off shady websites. This is small-office security with enterprise-level paranoia.

9.

WildFire support means it doesn't just block known threats—it learns new ones. The PA-220 can send unknown files to Palo Alto's cloud sandbox, receive verdicts, and update its security posture. Even the little guys get smarter by the second.

10.

Virtual wire, Layer 2, and Layer 3 deployments are all supported. Whether you want the PA-220 to act as a transparent filter, a switch, or a full-on routing gateway, it's ready. It's more flexible than a startup CTO wearing three hats.

11.

Routing support includes **static, OSPF, BGP**, and **policy-based forwarding**. That's right—this tiny box can handle dynamic routing protocols like it's auditioning for the data center drama club. It may not have 10G ports, but it sure has 10G dreams.

12.

High Availability is built in, with active/passive failover between two PA-220s. It's like a buddy system, but for firewalls—if one trips, the other picks up the slack. And yes, it's also **fanless**, which means no noise when it does.

13.

GlobalProtect VPN access is fully supported. Whether you're connecting remote workers or creating secure tunnels between branch sites, the PA-220 ensures encrypted, policy-enforced access without slowing things down to dial-up speeds.

14.

The **GUI** is Palo Alto's signature dashboard—modern, responsive, and logical. Small business owners can click through basic policies, and IT pros can go deep with rule customizations. Want CLI access? SSH and console are available for the power users.

15.

Panorama integration means you can manage multiple PA-220s from a centralized console. Roll out policies, push updates, gather logs—it's the perfect solution for distributed retail, satellite offices, or any company with a case of network sprawl.

16.

Logging is detailed and useful. It tracks traffic, threats, configuration changes, and URL access. You can export logs or forward them to a syslog server. If something weird happens, the PA-220 knows, timestamps it, and silently says, "Told you so."

17.

SSL decryption is supported, but manage your expectations. The PA-220 can inspect encrypted traffic, but don't point an entire office's video traffic through it during lunch hour. Use SSL policies wisely and target high-risk categories.

18.

Power consumption is gloriously low—**around 15 watts**. You could power it with a solar panel, a battery backup, or the positive vibes from your network admin. It's perfect for environmentally-conscious deployments or locations where kilowatts are costly.

19.

Captive portal support allows for web-based user authentication on guest Wi-Fi or shared networks. Whether you want to enforce logins, display terms and conditions, or just make sure Dave doesn't sneak in via his iPad again, the PA-220 has you covered.

20.

Role-based access control gives you fine-grained admin permissions. Let the local tech support handle log monitoring while your security team manages policy enforcement. Everyone gets what they need—nobody breaks anything accidentally.

21.

Licensing includes **Threat Prevention, URL Filtering, GlobalProtect**, and **WildFire**, all of which turn your little firewall into a next-gen powerhouse. Each subscription enhances what it can see, block, and learn—and yes, they're worth it.

22.

The PA-220 is the **ideal training unit**. Labs, tech demos, bootcamps—it's small, affordable, and gives students a full taste of Palo Alto's features without needing a 48-port switch and a six-foot stack of power strips.

23.

It's also a **remote branch hero**. Toss it into a small site, connect it back to headquarters, and enjoy centralized security with a low touch. No on-site staff needed—just good config and decent bandwidth.

24.

Even though it looks modest, the PA-220 is **still sold**, supported, and in use globally. It's not just holding the line—it's doing so silently, efficiently, and stylishly. It's basically James Bond if Bond spent more time configuring VPN tunnels.

25.

The PA-220 is cute. It's quiet. And it's **ridiculously competent**. For small deployments that want big protection, this is the box that proves you don't need to be loud to be lethal. It's the firewall equivalent of a silent assassin—if the assassin also offered URL filtering and GlobalProtect support.

Chapter 16: PA-820 – The Goldilocks Box

1.

Not too big, not too small, and juuust right—the **PA-820** is the firewall that Goldilocks would pick if she ran a secure branch office instead of a crime scene involving porridge theft. It hits the sweet spot between power and price, making it the go-to box when the PA-220 just can't keep up and the 3200 series feels a tad excessive.

2.

From the outside, it's got that clean, industrial Palo Alto look: fan vents, front-facing LEDs, and ports that say "Let's do some routing." But make no mistake—this 1U appliance isn't just attractive, it's a mid-sized marvel with serious next-gen features.

3.

With **8 Gigabit data ports**, **1 management port**, **1 console port**, and **2 HA ports**, the PA-820 supports high-availability configurations, segmented zones, and multiple ISP uplinks with elegance. In other words, it multitasks like a caffeinated network engineer.

4.

The performance metrics make it a true contender: **1.9 Gbps firewall throughput**, **800 Mbps of threat prevention**, and **192,000 concurrent sessions**. It doesn't just protect—it scales with you. Whether it's a growing branch office or a main office on a budget, the PA-820 holds the line.

5.

And yes—it runs **full PAN-OS** with **App-ID, User-ID, Content-ID, WildFire, and GlobalProtect**. There's no watered-down nonsense here. This is enterprise-class security for those who want premium-grade protection without breaking the CFO's heart.

6.

App-ID brings its usual magic, identifying and controlling applications by behavior instead of ports. You want to allow Microsoft Teams but block TikTok? No problem. Need to throttle Dropbox but let Google Drive run free? Done and done.

7.

User-ID helps you tie policy to people, not just IPs. It integrates with Active Directory and other identity sources, so when you need to trace a security violation, you're not chasing a MAC address—you're politely emailing Brenda in HR with a screenshot.

8.

Content-ID provides the deep inspection your network deserves. Malware, spyware, known bad URLs, DLP triggers—it blocks, logs, and neutralizes them in real time. And yes, it does this while still being snappy enough for video calls and VoIP.

9.

With **WildFire**, the PA-820 becomes part of Palo Alto's global intelligence network. It sends suspicious files to the cloud for sandbox analysis, learns from zero-day threats, and updates its own defenses—often before the threat makes the news.

10.

It supports **Layer 3, Layer 2, and virtual wire deployments**, allowing you to drop it into just about any architecture. Transparent bridge? No problem. Edge routing with NAT and QoS? Also fine. This box doesn't ask questions—it solves them.

11.

Routing is enterprise-grade: **OSPF, BGP, RIP, static**, and **policy-based routing** all work seamlessly. Even if your network diagram looks like it was drawn during turbulence, the PA-820 will find its way through.

12.

High Availability comes standard with active/passive failover, session sync, and link monitoring. If one unit takes a nap (or gets unplugged by an enthusiastic janitor), the other steps in like nothing ever happened—minus the error alert in your inbox.

13.

GlobalProtect VPN gives remote users secure, policy-enforced access to your network from anywhere on Earth—or from questionable Wi-Fi at coffee shops with overly creative SSIDs.

14.

The web-based **GUI** remains a joy: intuitive, modern, and powerful. For CLI fans, **SSH and console** access provide full command-line control. It's friendly to newbies and veteran firewall wranglers alike.

15.

Panorama integration is seamless. Whether you're managing one or one hundred PA-820s, you can push policy, pull logs, and monitor status from a single dashboard. The PA-820 might be small, but it plays well in large teams.

16.

Logging and reporting are detailed, accurate, and timestamped like they're ready for a court case. Whether you're auditing, troubleshooting, or just trying to figure out who downloaded 3GB of cat memes on a Tuesday, the PA-820 has the receipts.

17.

SSL decryption is fully supported. Just be strategic—don't go decrypting every Netflix session unless you enjoy slow complaints from marketing. Instead, use custom policies to inspect where it matters most: unknown traffic, file sharing, and unsanctioned applications.

18.

The **fan noise**? Manageable. Not silent, but not distracting either. It's not trying to make conversation—it just wants to inspect packets and be left alone. In a server closet or rack, it's practically a wallflower.

19.

Power draw hovers around **50–60 watts**, making it energy efficient while still capable of full deep packet inspection. You'll get top-tier protection without running up the utility bill—or overloading your UPS.

20.

Captive portal support lets you create guest logins, show splash pages, or enforce terms and conditions. Whether it's a coworking space, small campus, or client hotspot, you can make the access process secure, informative, and maybe even stylish.

21.

Role-based administration allows you to fine-tune what each admin can see or change. Your junior tech gets log access, your security engineer controls policy, and your boss can admire the pretty graphs without causing any network-wide catastrophes.

22.

Licensing follows Palo Alto's modular model: activate **Threat Prevention**, **URL Filtering**, **WildFire**, **GlobalProtect**, and any combination you need. Each one unlocks deeper visibility and stronger controls, letting you tailor the 820 to your environment.

23.

It's also a **lab favorite**, offering full next-gen features at a price and size ideal for training, testing, and building out demo environments. Whether you're teaching firewalls or breaking them (on purpose), the PA-820 is the perfect classroom assistant.

24.

Though midrange in classification, the PA-820 often punches above its weight. It handles multiple VLANs, policy layers, and advanced threat detection like a larger box—with fewer complaints and a smaller footprint.

25.

The **PA-820** is the firewall equivalent of a great cup of coffee: balanced, powerful, and absolutely necessary. It's perfect for small to medium deployments that want enterprise-grade protection without the enterprise-grade headaches. Goldilocks would be proud.

Chapter 17: PA-850 – Compact with a Kick

1.
Enter the **PA-850**: the firewall that kept the slim profile of its PA-800 series siblings but showed up to the network rack with protein shakes and a black belt in packet inspection. It's fast, full-featured, and fights way above its weight class. It doesn't need to brag—its logs speak for themselves.

2.
This sleek 1U unit looks like the PA-820's twin until you flip open the performance stats and realize you're dealing with a **mid-size monster**. It's not here to take up space—it's here to replace four other devices and make your other boxes question their self-worth.

3.
The **PA-850** includes **8 data ports**, **1 management port**, **1 console**, and **2 HA ports**, giving you the power to segment traffic, run dual WAN, enable HA, and still have room left over to guard your VLANs like a velvet-rope bouncer.

4.
Where it really kicks: **4.8 Gbps firewall throughput**, **2.1 Gbps of threat prevention**, and **384,000 concurrent sessions**. For a mid-sized unit, that's some serious swagger. It can easily support **100–300 users**, maybe more—depending on what you're letting them watch on YouTube.

5.
Like all its Palo Alto cousins, the PA-850 runs **full PAN-OS**, including **App-ID, User-ID, Content-ID, WildFire, and GlobalProtect**. It's not a stripped-down, budget build. It's a full-blown next-gen firewall hiding in a space-efficient frame.

6.
App-ID lets the 850 identify traffic by application, not by port or hope. Whether it's Slack, Signal, Steam, or some rogue Chrome extension, this firewall will see it, classify it, and give you the power to allow, limit, or punt it into the void.

7.
User-ID provides visibility into who's doing what—and when. Tie traffic to users, groups, or departments. If marketing accidentally triggers a threat alert during "lunch research," you'll know *exactly* who clicked what, when, and possibly why.

8.
Content-ID provides deep-packet inspection with advanced threat prevention. It filters malware, spyware, inappropriate content, and confidential data leaks—all while maintaining a smooth user experience. The PA-850 is the type of device that stops threats *and* latency complaints.

9.

With **WildFire** support, the PA-850 doesn't just defend—it **learns**. Suspicious files are sent to Palo Alto's cloud sandbox, detonated, analyzed, and documented. Verdicts are shared globally, giving your PA-850 a threat-hunting network bigger than most militaries.

10.

Deployment options? Naturally flexible. Use it in **Layer 3**, **Layer 2**, or **virtual wire mode**. Whether it's your main gateway, an internal segmentation device, or a transparent DPI filter dropped between two switches, the 850 fits the role like it was made for it. Because it was.

11.

Routing capabilities are enterprise-ready: **OSPF, BGP, RIP, static**, and **policy-based forwarding**. Even if your network spans across regions, clouds, or departments with questionable VLAN names, the 850 can route, NAT, and prioritize like a champ.

12.

And yes, **High Availability** is built in. Pair two PA-850s for active/passive failover, session synchronization, and high uptime. Your users won't notice a hiccup, but you'll get the satisfaction of knowing your firewall was built with a backup plan in mind.

13.

GlobalProtect VPN gives users secure remote access with full policy enforcement. Whether employees are working from home, abroad, or inside a coffee shop shaped like a lighthouse, the 850 ensures encrypted, identity-aware access.

14.

The **GUI** is the Palo Alto classic—clean, efficient, and robust. Graphs, logs, policies, and controls are easy to access and harder to mess up. For the CLI warriors, **SSH and console** access open up a world of control and troubleshooting nirvana.

15.

Panorama integration allows you to centrally manage multiple PA-850s, or mix and match with other Palo Alto firewalls. Push global policy, view logs, correlate threats—become the architect your network never knew it needed.

16.

Logging is fast, searchable, and thorough. Real-time traffic analysis, threat history, URL logs, system events, and configuration changes are all there, beautifully timestamped for the moment your manager says, "What happened yesterday at 3:47PM?"

17.

SSL decryption is supported and well-handled. The PA-850 can inspect encrypted traffic intelligently—just don't try to decrypt *everything* unless you also bought a support plan and earplugs for the complaints. Use categories and exceptions wisely.

18.

The **fan noise**? A bit louder than the PA-820, but still perfectly acceptable for closets, racks, or server rooms. Definitely not a dinner-table conversation piece unless you're into network noise ASMR.

19.

Power draw hovers around **70–90 watts**, offering a solid performance-to-energy ratio. Efficient, reliable, and unlikely to trip your UPS unless you installed it alongside a rack of space heaters and a cryptocurrency rig.

20.

Captive portal support allows guest login, BYOD enforcement, and splash-page authentication. Want to show users your logo, collect usernames, or force them to read your hilarious usage policy? The 850 says, "Right this way."

21.

Role-based admin controls let you assign permissions at the feature level. Give your help desk read-only access, your SOC team full policy control, and your interns… nothing. It's called smart delegation.

22.

Licensing follows Palo Alto's modular model: activate **Threat Prevention, WildFire, URL Filtering, GlobalProtect**, or a combination thereof. Each license adds a layer of functionality and peace of mind. Just don't forget to renew—threats don't care about expiration dates.

23.

It's also a favorite for **MSSPs**, **regional data centers**, and **larger branch offices**. Small enough to ship, powerful enough to centralize. The 850 handles complex, multi-zone environments without breaking a sweat or your support team.

24.

Despite being midrange in form factor, the PA-850 regularly surprises people with how much it can handle. From SD-WAN overlay protection to branch-level segmentation and everything in between, it's the little engine that *firewalls*.

25.

The **PA-850** is compact, capable, and kind of a show-off—but in the best way. It balances power, price, and polish better than almost anything in its class. Whether you're building a branch fortress or a smart satellite office, this is the box that kicks harder than it looks—and logs every punch.

Chapter 18: PA-3220 – The Modern Middleweight

1.

The **PA-3220** is the firewall equivalent of a lean boxer who never skips leg day—built for balance, power, and endurance. It landed in the Palo Alto lineup as the **entry point for the 3200 Series,** bringing enterprise-level punch to growing networks that need speed *and* brains.

2.

Visually, it's all business: a clean 1U design with purposeful venting, glowing status LEDs, and enough ports to suggest it's ready for some serious multitasking. It's not here to impress with looks. It's here to **inspect, block, and log** with cold precision.

3.

The PA-3220 is loaded with **16 ports** total: **8 Gigabit Ethernet (RJ-45)**, **8 SFP ports for fiber connections**, **1 management**, **1 console**, and **2 HA interfaces**. That kind of versatility lets it flex from copper to fiber without even blinking.

4.

Let's talk horsepower. It delivers **7.6 Gbps firewall throughput**, **3.4 Gbps threat prevention**, and **832,000 concurrent sessions**. For a 1U device, that's impressive. For a mid-size enterprise, that's a dream come true.

5.

As expected, it runs full **PAN-OS**, unlocking the Palo Alto power suite: **App-ID, User-ID, Content-ID, GlobalProtect**, and **WildFire**. There's no half-measures here. This is **next-gen security** in a form factor that fits in any rack without threatening your HVAC system.

6.

App-ID keeps application-level control smarter than ever. Instead of guessing based on ports, the PA-3220 identifies traffic based on behavior. Streaming site on port 443? It knows. DNS tunneling? Detected. TikTok over SSL? Get in line.

7.

User-ID connects users to traffic flows. Whether they're authenticated via LDAP, AD, or local sources, the PA-3220 ties actions to names. No more anonymous logs—just clear, traceable policy enforcement that keeps people accountable (especially Carl in Marketing).

8.

Content-ID brings inline deep-packet inspection with enterprise polish. It handles malware, spyware, file-type restrictions, DLP, and inappropriate URL categories like a seasoned bouncer. If it looks suspicious, it's flagged, blocked, and logged—fast.

9.

WildFire adds a layer of real-time threat intelligence. The PA-3220 ships unknown files to the cloud sandbox, detonates them in a safe virtual environment, and adjusts its behavior based on global intelligence. It's like having a malware psychic living inside your firewall.

10.

Deployment modes include **Layer 3, Layer 2, and virtual wire**. Whether you're inserting it transparently into a hybrid environment or using it as a gateway firewall for multiple zones, the 3220 adjusts without needing a complex ceremony or blood ritual.

11.

Routing protocols are fully supported: **OSPF, BGP, RIP, static routes**, and **PBF** (Policy-Based Forwarding). It's flexible enough for multi-site designs, hybrid cloud, or that "creative" campus topology that's evolved for 12 years without a diagram.

12.

High Availability is built-in and production-grade. You get active/passive failover, link monitoring, and session sync so seamless, your users won't even know something failed. Except you. You'll know. Because you'll get an email. Probably several.

13.

GlobalProtect ensures secure remote access with consistent policy enforcement. Whether employees are working from home, coworking spaces, or sketchy cafés with themed Wi-Fi, the 3220 enforces rules and decrypts encrypted tunnels like a pro.

14.

The **GUI** is Palo Alto's greatest hit album: clean, responsive, and built for both rookies and veterans. And yes, **CLI fans** can still SSH in, run packet captures, review route tables, and type "show session all" like it's a magic spell.

15.

With **Panorama**, managing multiple 3220s becomes simple. Push policy, sync updates, review global threat logs, and assign access roles from a single dashboard. It's command-and-control with style and substance.

16.

The PA-3220 logs like a novelist with a caffeine addiction. Threat logs, system events, configuration diffs, traffic history—it sees all, records all, and makes it exportable for your SIEM, your reports, and your favorite blaming exercise.

17.

SSL decryption is a core feature. With strong hardware acceleration, it can handle moderate encrypted inspection without choking. Define precise decryption policies and use categories to prioritize high-risk traffic. And maybe let Netflix live, just this once.

18.

Fan noise is present but tolerable. It hums with confidence but won't drown out your Zoom calls. Just don't rack it next to your meditation pod or inside a podcast studio. Unless your podcast is about packet inspection. In which case—perfect ambiance.

19.

Power draw lands between **100–150 watts**, which is impressive for something this fast. It's energy-conscious enough to run in distributed branch deployments without requiring a dedicated power plant.

20.

Captive portal features let you enforce user authentication on guest Wi-Fi or BYOD networks. Whether it's a splash screen, a legal disclaimer, or a friendly reminder not to stream "Fast & Furious 6" during work hours, the PA-3220 has you covered.

21.

Role-based access control lets you assign rights by user role. Let your SOC team dig into threat logs, your junior admin view stats, and your boss click dashboards that sparkle but can't delete anything. Governance made easy—and foolproof.

22.

Licensing options remain classic Palo Alto: **Threat Prevention, URL Filtering, GlobalProtect, WildFire**, and more. Buy what you need, scale as you grow, and sleep well knowing your security model grows with you, not against you.

23.

The PA-3220 is perfect for **regional offices, distributed enterprises, educational networks,** and **financial branches**. It's compact, powerful, and deceptively fast—like a librarian who moonlights as a martial arts instructor.

24.

Compared to its peers, the PA-3220 punches way above its size. It's often deployed in environments that expected to upgrade later—only to realize it's still going strong two years and three ransomware waves later.

25.

The **PA-3220** is the modern middleweight firewall: flexible, formidable, and future-ready. If you need deep inspection, reliable throughput, and security intelligence without stepping into data-center overkill, this is your go-to. It won't just guard your perimeter—it'll **outthink** anything that tries to cross it.

Chapter 19: PA-3250 – Midrange Hero Mode Activated

1.

The **PA-3250** didn't walk into the midrange market—it **drop-kicked** its way in. This firewall took everything the PA-3220 was doing well and turned the dial from "pretty good" to "did it just inspect a gigabit stream while decrypting and laughing at a botnet?"

2.

This unit is the **middle sibling of the PA-3200 Series**, but it refuses to blend in. Built for high-throughput environments with complex application flows, the PA-3250 is the hero you call when your network gets a little too real for entry-level firewalls.

3.

Physically, it looks like its 3220 and 3260 siblings—sleek 1U design, status LEDs, and airflow grills that whisper, "I work hard, but I stay cool." It fits easily into any standard rack and blends in… until it starts making security decisions faster than you can say "zero trust."

4.

Port-wise, you get **16 total interfaces**: **8 Gigabit RJ-45**, **8 SFP**, plus the standard **management, console**, and **2 HA** ports. This thing's network flexibility is ideal for growing networks, dual-WAN setups, or multi-zone segmentation with a dash of elegance.

5.

Performance-wise, it means business: **16.2 Gbps firewall throughput**, **8.3 Gbps threat prevention**, and **1.4 million concurrent sessions**. That's not just fast—it's **data center flirtation** speeds in a mid-sized package.

6.

Naturally, it runs full **PAN-OS**, unlocking **App-ID, User-ID, Content-ID, WildFire**, and **GlobalProtect**. You get the complete suite of next-gen security tools—all packaged in a device that feels like it should cost way more than it does.

7.

App-ID shines here, allowing granular control over apps at wire speed. Whether it's blocking non-business applications, throttling bandwidth vampires, or shaping traffic by category, the 3250 handles it all without breaking a sweat—or a session.

8.

User-ID brings that human context. Tie users to policies via Active Directory, LDAP, RADIUS, or SAML. When you need to track down who tried to upload your quarterly earnings spreadsheet to a public file share, the 3250 already has a name—and a log.

9.

Content-ID is where the real magic happens. Inline antivirus, spyware blocking, file-type filtering, and URL classification ensure that even the cleverest malware gets shut down at layer 7. This is the bouncer that asks malware for its ID and then tears it in half.

10.

WildFire integration provides zero-day protection by submitting suspicious files to the cloud for sandboxing. Results are distributed globally in minutes. Your 3250 doesn't just defend your network—it makes *other* 3250s smarter too. Firewalls helping firewalls? That's community.

11.

Deployment is flexible: **Layer 3**, **Layer 2**, **virtual wire**, or a mix of them all. Whether you're segmenting a building, bridging VLANs, or creating an east-west inspection zone, the PA-3250 adapts like a shapeshifter with a config file.

12.

Routing protocols? You've got them: **OSPF, BGP, RIP, static**, and **policy-based forwarding**. It's as comfortable as an edge gateway as it is buried in your core. Just be ready to fall in love with its deterministic routing behavior.

13.

High Availability is enterprise-grade. Active/passive setups with full session synchronization ensure that failovers are invisible to end users. You'll see it in the logs, but they'll never know. Just how you like it.

14.

Remote access is seamless with **GlobalProtect VPN**. Whether your users are at home, traveling, or connecting from 4G hotspots in the middle of nowhere, they get secure access with endpoint compliance checks and all the same policy enforcement they'd get in the office.

15.

The **GUI** is intuitive, responsive, and loaded with insight. Application usage, top threats, blocked attempts, and rule hits are all presented with crisp visuals. And for CLI purists, **SSH** delivers the deep diagnostic magic you crave—one `show session all` at a time.

16.

Panorama integration is flawless. Whether you're managing a handful of firewalls or orchestrating policy across continents, Panorama and the PA-3250 get along beautifully. Global security posture, meet real-time enforcement.

17.

Logging is robust, fast, and insightful. Every allowed, denied, inspected, or squashed packet is timestamped and searchable. You want forensic-level detail? The 3250 is basically a packet historian with trust issues.

18.

SSL decryption is strong and optimized. With its beefy hardware and smart inspection pipeline, the PA-3250 can decrypt at scale. Create precise policies to target suspicious categories and avoid triggering a mutiny from your streaming-addicted coworkers.

19.

Fan noise is present but refined—let's call it "data center chic." It's not whisper-quiet, but it's nowhere near 5060 roar levels. Think "I'm working hard over here" energy, not "I'm revving for takeoff."

20.

Power draw averages around **170–200 watts**, giving it a great efficiency-to-performance ratio. It's the kind of appliance you can deploy in a rack without needing to double your HVAC settings or kiss your UPS goodbye.

21.

Captive portal capabilities let you enforce guest policies, display login prompts, and even serve up customized splash pages. Great for branch offices, Wi-Fi zones, and making interns read your hilarious "Acceptable Use" policy.

22.

Role-based admin controls ensure your team doesn't accidentally nuke production while trying to change log retention settings. Let junior staff view logs, give your security engineers full policy access, and let managers... just watch the pretty graphs.

23.

Licensing is modular: activate **Threat Prevention**, **URL Filtering**, **WildFire**, **GlobalProtect**, or bundle them all. Each license adds deep functionality, turning the PA-3250 into more of a threat-sniffing oracle than a firewall.

24.

You'll find this model in **regional data centers**, **large campuses**, and **multi-site enterprise cores**. It's fast, future-ready, and engineered to take traffic spikes in stride. It doesn't panic—it filters.

25.

The **PA-3250** is the unsung hero of the midrange. It's not oversized or overpriced—but it absolutely over-delivers. For organizations that need application control, deep inspection, and high-speed prevention in one rack unit, this is your firewall. Midrange hero mode: **activated**.

Chapter 20: PA-3260 – IDS for the Evolving Edge

1.

If the PA-3250 is the hero of midrange networks, then the **PA-3260** is the **strategic commander** —faster, stronger, and smarter, designed for evolving edge environments where *everything* is talking to *everything*. It doesn't just inspect—it **orchestrates** and **dominates**.

2.

Housed in a standard 1U chassis, the PA-3260 might look like its 3200 siblings, but internally, it's a **performance predator**. This is the top tier of the series, meant for large branch offices, mid-sized data centers, or enterprises that think gigabit is cute.

3.

You get **16 network ports: 8x RJ-45, 8x SFP**, plus your **management**, **console**, and **HA** ports. That's enough to carve out DMZs, segment zones like a VLAN ninja, and keep redundant ISPs in check without breaking a sweat—or your cabling strategy.

4.

Let's talk numbers. The PA-3260 delivers **19.2 Gbps firewall throughput, 9.5 Gbps of threat prevention**, and a whopping **2.4 million concurrent sessions**. That's enterprise performance in a form factor that doesn't require a forklift or a monthly power bill the size of your mortgage.

5.

Of course, it runs full-blown **PAN-OS**. You get the full suite: **App-ID, User-ID, Content-ID, WildFire, GlobalProtect**, and even **advanced routing and segmentation capabilities**. No watered-down firmware here—this is the good stuff, in full.

6.

App-ID is like an application profiler with attitude. The 3260 recognizes traffic based on behavior, not port numbers or false promises. Whether it's Facebook wrapped in HTTPS or a sneaky peer-to-peer app, this firewall spots it and takes appropriate action—like a digital parole officer.

7.

User-ID integrates identity into your policies. Instead of "who's 192.168.20.42?", you'll know it's **Sharon from Finance**, and yes—she's trying to upload confidential documents to a third-party FTP site. Again. Time for a chat, Sharon.

8.

Content-ID brings in inline antivirus, file-type control, data loss prevention, spyware blocking, and URL filtering. It inspects packets like they owe it money—and then sends them to quarantine if they get snarky.

9.

WildFire keeps things proactive. The PA-3260 can offload suspicious files to the cloud sandbox, detonate them in isolation, analyze behavior, and receive verdicts within minutes. You don't just block malware—you help defeat it across every WildFire-enabled firewall globally.

10.

Deployment modes include **Layer 3, Layer 2, virtual wire**, and yes, **hybrid scenarios**. The 3260 doesn't care how weird your topology is—it adapts, secures, and moves on. It's the Swiss Army knife of firewalls, minus the bottle opener.

11.

On the routing side, you've got full support for **BGP, OSPF, RIP, static routes**, and **PBF (Policy-Based Forwarding)**. Use it at your core, edge, or in tandem with SD-WAN overlays—it doesn't flinch. It routes, NATs, and classifies with dignity.

12.

High Availability? Naturally. Active/passive failover, full session sync, link monitoring, and health checks are built-in. If one 3260 goes belly-up, the other steps in like a professional stunt double—zero downtime, zero drama.

13.

GlobalProtect VPN provides remote access that's secure, policy-enforced, and identity-aware. Whether your employees are at home, on a train, or working from a hammock in Tulum, the 3260 keeps things encrypted and compliant.

14.

The **GUI** is pure Palo Alto: sleek, colorful, and way more user-friendly than most "enterprise" dashboards. For the purists, **CLI via SSH** delivers surgical access to routing tables, session captures, and all your "let me troubleshoot this manually" needs.

15.

Panorama integration is seamless. Manage dozens — or hundreds — of 3260s from one console. Push policies globally, aggregate logs, create reports, and look like a wizard during security meetings. Centralized management has never been this slick.

16.

Logging? Like a court stenographer with a photographic memory. Every session, threat, connection, and config change is logged, timestamped, and ready to hand over to your SIEM — or your boss when something gets weird at 3AM.

17.

SSL decryption is no longer optional, and the PA-3260 handles it like a champion. It inspects encrypted traffic at scale, pulling the curtains back on those "unknown" sessions so you can apply your threat prevention where it actually matters.

18.

Fan noise is present, but reasonable — think "low white noise" rather than "vacuum cleaner on Red Bull." It belongs in a rack, not on your desk, but it won't scream for attention unless something's truly wrong.

19.

Power usage lands between **200–250 watts**, which is impressive given what it's doing under the hood. Energy-efficient, reliable, and unlikely to blow a breaker during peak hours. Unless you've installed it next to a space heater. Don't do that.

20.

Captive portal support makes guest and BYOD management easy. Redirect users to login portals, collect credentials, splash your branding, and enforce temporary access policies without deploying a separate NAC system.

21.

Role-based access control allows you to define exactly who can touch what. Let junior admins poke around logs, give senior engineers full config access, and keep auditors in their read-only sandbox where they can't break things. You'll thank yourself later.

22.

Licensing is modular and unlocks serious power: **Threat Prevention**, **WildFire**, **GlobalProtect**, **URL Filtering**, and **DNS Security** are all part of the package. Activate what you need and scale up as the threats evolve — which they will.

23.

The PA-3260 is ideal for **enterprise branches**, **university cores**, **regional offices**, and **multi-cloud edge deployments**. It's fast enough to inspect real traffic and smart enough to do it **without** becoming a bottleneck or needing babysitting.

24.

In real-world use, the 3260 often outperforms its advertised specs—especially when configured properly and kept on a healthy diet of updates and WildFire intelligence. It's a plug-and-play genius for networks ready to move past traditional IDS thinking.

25.

The **PA-3260** is not just an IDS. It's a **modern edge enforcer**, an **application-aware sentinel**, and a **cloud-connected defender**. When you're ready to secure your perimeter *and* your future, this is the box that's already watching, learning, and logging—just waiting for the next packet to prove itself.

Chapter 21: PA-3410 – Brains, Brawn, and Bandwidth

1.

The **PA-3410** is what happens when Palo Alto engineers stare at a PA-3200 series and say, "More." More power, more visibility, more threat detection—wrapped in a sleek 1U chassis that quietly dares malware to try something. It's not just a firewall. It's a **full-blown security platform on turbo mode**.

2.

Let's get this out of the way: the PA-3410 is part of Palo Alto's **next-gen hardware refresh**, designed to tackle the modern security landscape where cloud, hybrid, and IoT madness coexist in glorious chaos. It's built for today's edge—and tomorrow's traffic spikes.

3.

Physically, the unit looks clean, sturdy, and ready for action. It features **16 network interfaces**: **8 RJ-45**, **8 SFP**, plus **management**, **console**, and **HA ports**. If your rack likes balance, symmetry, and utility, the 3410 fits right in—like a well-dressed ninja.

4.

Performance-wise, this one's a beast: **19 Gbps firewall throughput, 9.4 Gbps threat prevention**, and **3 million concurrent sessions**. That's enough to handle branch cores, regional HQs, and edge deployments without batting a fan blade.

5.

As expected, it runs the full **PAN-OS**, meaning you get **App-ID, User-ID, Content-ID, GlobalProtect, WildFire**, and even **Machine Learning–based threat analysis**. It's basically a security analyst with a silicon backbone and no lunch breaks.

6.

App-ID remains the star of the show, identifying traffic based on behavior—not just ports or guesses. Whether it's encrypted Zoom calls, evasive browser plugins, or shadow IT apps, the PA-3410 sees it, labels it, and gives you the power to throttle or block it on sight.

7.

User-ID ties traffic to identities—LDAP, Active Directory, local users, or even cloud identity providers. You'll always know who downloaded what, where they sent it, and whether it violated the Acceptable Use Policy you know nobody actually reads.

8.

Content-ID delivers real-time inline protection from malware, exploits, phishing attempts, and data leaks. Whether it's email attachments, sneaky URLs, or encrypted payloads trying to exfiltrate files at midnight, the 3410 is watching—and logging—with judgment.

9.

WildFire integration means the 3410 can send suspicious files to Palo Alto's cloud sandbox for behavioral analysis. Verdicts are shared globally in real time, so your firewall isn't just defending your network—it's **contributing to a worldwide threat suppression network**.

10.

Deployment options include **Layer 3, Layer 2, and virtual wire**, making it flexible enough to act as a gateway, bridge, or transparent inline monitor. However weird your architecture is, the 3410 won't judge. It'll secure it and smile quietly.

11.

Routing support includes **OSPF, BGP, RIP, static**, and **policy-based routing**, enabling complex segmentation, dynamic pathing, and zero-trust enforcement across departments, regions, or that one server room that's still running Novell.

12.

High Availability support is standard. Active/passive failover, session sync, heartbeat monitoring—it's all here. When one unit has a bad firmware day, the other takes over instantly like a well-trained understudy with a laminated playbook.

13.

GlobalProtect VPN is fully supported and deeply integrated. Whether your users are remote, hybrid, or hopping between networks like caffeinated squirrels, the 3410 keeps access secure, compliant, and policy-driven.

14.

The **GUI** is modern, elegant, and powerful—great for visual learners and dashboard junkies alike. And for CLI fans? **SSH access** provides all the gritty detail, packet captures, and debugging tools your terminal-loving soul desires.

15.

Panorama support lets you manage multiple PA-3410s from a central console. Push rules, collect logs, enforce uniform policies, and generate cross-site reports like a multi-office security architect with an all-seeing eye.

16.

Logging and reporting are surgical. Every connection, policy match, blocked threat, and configuration tweak is recorded. The 3410's memory is long—and its timestamps are accurate to the millisecond. Perfect for audits, forensics, or proving your innocence.

17.

SSL decryption is handled with impressive grace. The 3410 inspects encrypted traffic at scale, prioritizing security without tanking performance. Configure smart exceptions, decrypt the right traffic, and enjoy X-ray vision through HTTPS.

18.

Fan noise? Acceptable. Not whisper-quiet, but it hums confidently. This is not the device to put under your desk unless you like sleeping to the sound of DPI in action. It belongs in a rack, where it can breathe and do its work without interruption.

19.

Power draw lands in the **220–270 watt range**, depending on throughput and active subscriptions. It's a powerful box, but efficient—just don't try to run it off a wall plug next to your space heater and mini-fridge.

20.

Captive portal is available for BYOD, guests, or restricted zones. You can customize login pages, enforce identity before access, and even add your company logo—because branding matters, even when users are just trying to check their email.

21.

Role-based access control gives you granular admin delegation. Let the intern view logs, the engineer tune policies, and the security director click "export report" while looking thoughtful. Everyone gets what they need—no more, no less.

22.

Licensing is as flexible as ever: activate **Threat Prevention, DNS Security, URL Filtering, GlobalProtect**, and **WildFire** à la carte. Each subscription unlocks capabilities that level up your security posture—and yes, they're worth every penny.

23.

Ideal use cases include **enterprise edge deployments**, **regional data centers**, **high-performance campuses**, and **mid-sized cloud egress zones**. The PA-3410 doesn't just keep up —it **defines** what secure edge performance looks like.

24.

This firewall is built for organizations that want inspection, enforcement, and prevention—without bottlenecks or blank stares from their SOC. It's the perfect mix of speed, control, and next-gen context, all wrapped in a deceptively quiet shell.

25.

The **PA-3410** is brains, brawn, and bandwidth in a balanced, beautiful box. It's the security appliance you buy when you need your firewall to do more than just block ports—it needs to **understand traffic**, **protect users**, and **scale intelligently**. If firewalls were superheroes, the 3410 would wear a cape made of VLANs and carry a sword forged from threat logs.

Chapter 22: PA-5250 – Speed, Space, and Security

1.

When your network gets too fast for entry-level firewalls and too complex for a mid-range box, the **PA-5250** steps up like a champion sprinter in full-body armor. It's designed for high-speed data centers, large-scale enterprise edges, and any deployment where throughput and security can't be mutually exclusive.

2.

This isn't just another firewall. It's part of the **PA-5200 Series**, which was created to tackle explosive bandwidth demands, unpredictable threat vectors, and admins who've seen too much and want **everything visible, fast, and locked down**.

3.

The PA-5250 lives in a **2U chassis**, signaling from the jump that it means business. It comes stacked with **12 SFP/SFP+ interfaces**, **4 RJ-45 ports**, **dual power supplies**, and of course, **HA and management interfaces**. It's a rackspace investment that pays off in performance dividends.

4.

Let's get the performance stats out of the way because they're gorgeous: **36 Gbps firewall throughput**, **17 Gbps threat prevention**, and **6 million concurrent sessions**. That's enough to keep up with gigabit-hungry environments **and** deep packet inspection **at the same time**.

5.

Like all next-gen Palo Altos, it runs the full **PAN-OS** experience: **App-ID, User-ID, Content-ID, WildFire, GlobalProtect**, and a host of advanced security services that let you slice and dice traffic with policy surgical precision.

6.

App-ID on the 5250 is more than just app detection—it's **app awareness at wire speed**. It can identify evasive, encrypted, or nested traffic patterns and classify them so you know *exactly* what's running in your network—and what *shouldn't* be.

7.

User-ID ties traffic to real human beings, not just IPs. With seamless integration to Active Directory, RADIUS, and cloud identity providers, it tells you **who did what**, not just where it came from. Accountability is just a log entry away.

8.

Content-ID does what it does best: filter, block, and protect. You get inline antivirus, anti-spyware, URL filtering, file blocking, and DLP—all delivered with the efficiency of a bouncer who knows who's on the list and who's bringing malware.

9.

WildFire transforms this appliance from a reactive tool to a **global threat intelligence node**. Suspicious files are analyzed in the cloud, detonated in sandbox environments, and verdicts are shared worldwide—so your firewall stays current on threats **that haven't even hit the news yet**.

10.

The PA-5250 supports **Layer 2, Layer 3, and virtual wire deployments**, so you can drop it into a network invisibly or make it the center of your universe. It plays well with others, even if it's the smartest box in the room.

11.

Routing is advanced and expected: full support for **BGP, OSPF, RIP, static**, and **policy-based forwarding**. Whether your topology is beautifully flat or disturbingly three-dimensional, the 5250 will route packets, enforce policies, and hold the line.

12.

Of course, it supports **High Availability**. Active/passive failover with stateful session sync, link monitoring, and heartbeats means that downtime is minimized. This thing is built for **five nines**, and it's not shy about it.

13.

GlobalProtect VPN is fully supported, enabling secure, encrypted tunnels from anywhere in the world. Your remote users won't know how lucky they are. Their devices are scanned, validated, and allowed through—*only* if they meet your exacting standards.

14.

The **GUI** is classic Palo Alto: polished, efficient, and surprisingly non-frustrating for something this powerful. And for the shell warriors? **SSH CLI access** lets you go deep—pull packet captures, inspect session states, and surgically tweak configs like a command-line surgeon.

15.

Panorama integration is a given. When you're deploying 5250s across multiple sites, having centralized policy control, real-time visibility, and uniform updates is not just helpful—it's **necessary**. And the 5250 speaks Panorama fluently.

16.

Logging is ridiculously detailed. Every session, drop, threat, and policy match is documented, timestamped, and ready for your SIEM. If you don't know what happened, it's because you haven't looked at the logs yet—not because the 5250 missed it.

17.

SSL decryption is handled with confidence. It can inspect encrypted traffic at scale, allowing you to create category-based exceptions, prioritize decryption targets, and avoid becoming your own bottleneck.

18.

Fan noise? Moderate. It's a 2U unit with serious internals, so yes—it hums. But in a data center, it blends right in with the sonic backdrop of uptime, airflow, and digital destiny. You won't notice it unless you're hugging the rack.

19.

Power consumption? Expect around **400–500 watts**, depending on traffic and enabled features. It's not a lightweight, but with that much power, it earns every electron. And yes, it plays nicely with dual PSUs and your clean power setup.

20.
Captive portal support is there and ready. Great for guest access, BYOD, and semi-trusted zones. Redirect unauthenticated users, throw your logo on a splash page, and add a disclaimer that nobody reads but everyone has to click through.

21.
Role-based access control is enterprise-ready. You can restrict access down to the feature level. Your junior admins get to click buttons. Your senior engineers get the keys to the kingdom. Your CISO gets a dashboard and plausible deniability.

22.
Licensing includes the usual Palo Alto goodness: **Threat Prevention, WildFire, URL Filtering, GlobalProtect, DNS Security**, and **Advanced Threat Prevention**. Activate what you need now and scale as your paranoia (or traffic) grows.

23.
Use cases? Think **data center perimeters**, **campus cores**, **cloud egress points**, and **enterprise security hubs**. This is where fast traffic meets smart inspection — and nothing gets through without answering a few very uncomfortable questions.

24.
For organizations dealing with encrypted threats, lateral movement, and bandwidth that makes lesser firewalls cry, the PA-5250 is a godsend. It has the muscle to go fast and the brain to go deep — **without compromise**.

25.
The **PA-5250** is what happens when speed, space, and security find perfect harmony. It's the high-performance defender you deploy when the stakes are high, the packets are flying, and the CFO just asked, "Are we secure?" With this box in your rack, the answer is an effortless, confident "Yes."

Chapter 23: PA-5260 – Because Gigabit Isn't Enough

1.
When your network laughs at gigabit links and your users treat HD video like email, you don't call for a firewall — you call for the **PA-5260**. This isn't just a next-gen firewall. It's a **data center enforcer**, built for organizations that treat 10Gbps as a warm-up.

2.
The **PA-5260** is the elder sibling in the PA-5200 Series and comes in hot with **more throughput, more session capacity, and more swagger** than most devices on your network. It doesn't merely keep up with high-speed environments — it **owns** them.

3.

It takes up **2U of rack space**, and every inch is justified. With **12 SFP/SFP+ ports**, **4 copper RJ-45 ports**, **2 HA interfaces**, and redundant power supplies, the 5260 is ready for whatever wiring diagram your architect dreamed up during a caffeine binge.

4.

Let's hit the numbers that matter: **58 Gbps firewall throughput**, **27 Gbps threat prevention**, and **12 million concurrent sessions**. That's not "big enough." That's "bring it on." If your traffic spikes break lesser firewalls, the 5260 says, "Was that all?"

5.

It runs the full-fat version of **PAN-OS**, with no corners cut. **App-ID, User-ID, Content-ID, WildFire, GlobalProtect**, **DNS Security**, and **Advanced Threat Prevention** are all onboard. It's the software suite of champions running on hardware that can keep up.

6.

App-ID at 58 Gbps? You bet. The PA-5260 classifies traffic in real time, even when apps hide in SSL tunnels, change ports like socks, or behave like they're trying to get past security at a nightclub. This firewall sees them. All of them.

7.

User-ID scales beautifully in large orgs, mapping millions of sessions to identities with no visible lag. Whether your directory is on-prem, hybrid, cloud-native, or duct-taped together with scripts and hope, the 5260 makes it work.

8.

Content-ID performs malware inspection, data leak prevention, URL filtering, and file-type control—at frightening speeds. Other firewalls pause for breath during DPI. This one does it mid-stride, on a treadmill, while humming Beethoven.

9.

And **WildFire**? Fully integrated and lightning fast. Unknown files are analyzed in the cloud and verdicts are delivered within minutes, empowering the 5260 to block threats that don't even have names yet. Zero-day? Meet zero-chance.

10.

You can deploy the PA-5260 as a **Layer 3 gateway**, a **Layer 2 bridge**, a **virtual wire**, or some hybrid monstrosity your infrastructure team insists is "the future." It adapts. It defends. It never complains.

11.

Routing is enterprise-grade and then some: **BGP, OSPF, RIP, static**, and **policy-based forwarding** come standard. The 5260 can handle multi-site routing, SD-WAN overlays, cloud pathing, and whatever topology your CTO cooked up while experimenting with microsegmentation.

12.

High Availability? Of course. Dual 5260s can operate in active/passive mode with seamless failover. When one goes down—planned or otherwise—the other picks up the baton like it was always running the show.

13.

GlobalProtect VPN access is here in full force. Whether you're supporting a hundred remote users or ten thousand, the PA-5260 offers secure, identity-based access with endpoint posture checks and a "no funny business" attitude.

14.

The **GUI** is Palo Alto's greatest hits album—refined, fast, and filled with meaningful dashboards. The CLI, accessed via SSH, provides detailed visibility and low-level control for engineers who speak fluent terminal and trust no mouse.

15.

Panorama integration is essential at this scale, and the PA-5260 plays its part flawlessly. Global policy push, log aggregation, cross-device rule deployment—it turns enterprise security orchestration into a well-oiled machine.

16.

Logs? Oh yes. With millions of sessions per second, the 5260 logs with precision, speed, and grace. You can correlate threats, view session histories, and build incident timelines with forensic confidence. It doesn't just store data—it tells stories.

17.

SSL decryption is enterprise-grade and hardware-assisted. You can safely inspect encrypted traffic without bottlenecks—as long as you define decryption policies wisely. Use categories, trusted root exceptions, and common sense. Or don't. The 5260 will still try to keep up.

18.

Fan noise? Let's say it's "confident." This isn't a desktop device—it's a high-performance security engine. In a rack, it blends in. In an office, it politely suggests you put it somewhere with airflow and earplugs.

19.

Power draw ranges from **500–600 watts**, depending on configuration and workload. It's not a lightweight, but if you're running 50 Gbps through your firewall, this is the electrical diet you signed up for.

20.

Captive portal support gives you an easy way to authenticate users, present policies, or brand your guest access network. Because nothing says "security with style" like a custom splash page and a legal disclaimer nobody reads.

21.

Role-based access control is a must at this level. Define exactly who can view, change, and deploy. Let interns view logs, engineers manage policies, and execs stare at pretty dashboards and feel involved. Everyone wins.

22.

Licensing is powerful and stackable. **Threat Prevention**, **Advanced URL Filtering**, **DNS Security**, **WildFire**, **IoT Security**, and **GlobalProtect** are all available. Pick what you need, and activate more when your risk tolerance inevitably plummets.

23.

Use cases include **high-volume data centers**, **cloud egress points**, **intercontinental enterprise networks**, and **large service provider cores**. If you need to defend your kingdom while your subjects stream, upload, download, and share, this is your shield.

24.

The PA-5260 was designed for high velocity and high intelligence. It doesn't blink when traffic floods or threats spike. It just filters, inspects, logs, and protects—faster than attackers can pivot and quieter than your budget meeting.

25.

The **PA-5260** isn't about keeping up—it's about staying *ahead*. It's the firewall you deploy when you've got serious traffic, serious threats, and a serious need for **speed with context**. Because in today's world, gigabit isn't enough. And with this box, it doesn't have to be.

Chapter 25: PA-7530 – Apex Predator in the PAN Jungle

1.

Welcome to the top of the Palo Alto food chain: the **PA-7530**, the apex predator, the alpha of advanced threat prevention, and the firewall that even malware talks about in hushed tones. It's more than a device—it's **a security ecosystem in a 5U chassis**, engineered to dominate hyperscale environments where packet flows resemble Niagara Falls. The PA-7530 is where you go when 100 Gbps isn't "a lot"—it's "Monday morning." If the PA-5450 is a beast, the 7530 is **a sentient firewall AI wrapped in titanium armor**. It doesn't blink, it doesn't flinch, and it certainly doesn't slow down. This is not a box you buy—this is a **decision you commit to**. Designed for the largest enterprises, ISPs, content delivery networks, and borderless cloud fortresses, the 7530 represents the pinnacle of Palo Alto's hardware evolution. Its competitors don't run against it—they run **away** from it. You don't test the 7530's limits. You adapt your infrastructure to **handle it**. It's fast. It's smart. It's the future.

2.

Physically, it's a marvel. The **PA-7530** lives in a **5U modular chassis**, equipped with redundant **management controllers**, **power supplies**, **fan trays**, and **network processing cards** that slide in like precision weapons. Its vertical card orientation optimizes airflow while looking intimidatingly futuristic. It's one of the few firewalls that makes data center staff **pause and admire** before deployment. You don't just rack this beast—you **announce it**. LEDs light up like a starship ready for takeoff. Cable management becomes a work of art. Power draw is significant, but justified. The build quality screams industrial-grade with zero tolerance for failure. It was designed to run hot, hard, and **forever**.

3.

Now for the meat: **Performance numbers that make grown engineers tear up**. We're talking **2.3 Tbps firewall throughput, 1.1 Tbps threat prevention**, and a jaw-dropping **300 million concurrent sessions**. That's not "room to grow"—that's "room for the world." You could route, inspect, decrypt, and neutralize **simultaneous nation-scale traffic** without buffering. Need full-pipe TLS inspection while filtering 30,000 applications? It yawns. Want to log every connection, every attempt, every anomaly while maintaining line-rate speed? That's called **Tuesday** for the PA-7530. This thing **redefines scale**.

4.

PAN-OS? Naturally. Full-stack, no compromise. The 7530 supports **App-ID, User-ID, Content-ID, WildFire, DNS Security, Advanced Threat Prevention**, and every security blade Palo Alto offers—plus room for features that haven't been invented yet. It's your **multi-tenant, hybrid-cloud, AI-assisted perimeter powerhouse**.

5.

App-ID runs at warp speed. It classifies millions of application instances with **real-time signature recognition, machine learning**, and **adaptive behavioral profiling**. Apps that try to disguise themselves get outed instantly. Port hopping? Obfuscation? Encryption? Irrelevant. The 7530 peels back layers faster than your SIEM refreshes.

6.

User-ID is built for federated identity chaos. Connect to hybrid Active Directory, Azure AD, Okta, LDAP, RADIUS, or a homemade SAML portal written during a hackathon. The 7530 correlates identities across clouds and continents, giving you policy based on **who**, not just where or what.

7.

Content-ID is next-level. It inspects every byte for malware, APTs, phishing payloads, malicious scripts, file type misuse, and data leaks. It does **DLP, compliance enforcement**, and **sandbox pre-filtering**—simultaneously, at terabit speeds. It's not filtering anymore—it's **packet judgment**.

8.

WildFire is practically sentient here. Unknown files are instantly submitted for analysis, detonated in dynamic sandbox environments, and verdicts are enforced before your screen finishes loading. With **inline ML**, the 7530 doesn't just block bad files—it **predicts them**.

9.

SSL decryption? Buckle up. The PA-7530 can decrypt **massive volumes of encrypted traffic** without blinking. It inspects TLS sessions, applies policy, enforces threat prevention, and maintains compliance even in a post-quantum-threat era. Use it wisely—it has **X-ray vision** for your traffic.

10.

Routing? Yes, and then some. BGP, OSPF, RIP, static, policy-based—you name it. Multicast support, route redistribution, multi-tenant segmentation—check, check, check. Whether you're bridging continents or segmenting blast zones, the PA-7530 routes **like a carrier core router wearing a badge**.

11.

High Availability? The only acceptable option. Clustered 7530s operate in **active/active or active/passive**, with synchronized sessions, redundant paths, and failover smoother than your change management docs. You can replace a line card during traffic flow. The system doesn't flinch.

12.

GlobalProtect? Oh, it scales. Thousands—tens of thousands—of remote users can connect simultaneously, with full policy enforcement, endpoint posture checks, and geo-aware routing. If your VPN needs a VPN, you should've bought a 7530.

13.

Management interfaces are polished, responsive, and shockingly lightweight considering what's going on under the hood. Full API support, CLI tools, RESTful services, and compatibility with **Terraform, Ansible**, and **Panorama** make it a DevSecOps dream.

14.

Speaking of **Panorama**, it's mandatory at this level. Centralized control, log aggregation, rule templating, and multi-device orchestration aren't just nice—they're **required**. If the 7530 is the sword, Panorama is the **scabbard that makes it deadly and scalable**.

15.

Logging is comprehensive. Real-time session stats, threat logs, DNS lookups, command traces, config changes—it's **security observability, quantified and actionable**. You can feed it into any SIEM and still keep a local copy because… why not?

16.

Machine Learning elevates the 7530 to new heights. From inline malware detection to zero-day prediction and behavioral anomaly scoring, the 7530 **learns with every packet**, every alert, every blocked exploit. It's evolving—*constantly*.

17.

And it supports **IoT Security, 5G-aware policy, container-native traffic inspection**, and **multi-cloud visibility**. It's the first Palo Alto box that feels like it was built **for what's coming**, not just what's here.

18.

Power draw hovers around **1700–2000 watts** fully loaded. It needs dedicated cooling and high-availability power architecture. If your rack can't handle it, the 7530 won't apologize. It came to play. You came to protect.

19.

Fan noise? Jet engine adjacent. If you're racking this thing in a room with humans, add soundproofing or prepare to explain why your firewall sounds like takeoff at O'Hare.

20.

Ports? It has all the ports. 100GbE, 25GbE, 10GbE, copper, fiber—it supports a range of line cards that let you architect your dream network. Or nightmare. It can handle both.

21.

Licensing is extensive: **Threat Prevention, WildFire, Advanced URL Filtering, DNS Security, GlobalProtect, AIOps**, and more. Each subscription unlocks **another layer of menace-blocking brilliance**. You're not just buying throughput—you're buying vision.

22.

Ideal use cases? **National telecoms, hyperscale cloud platforms, border security, intercontinental MPLS nodes**, and **nexus points in the global internet fabric**. This is not a branch firewall. This is **border control with teeth**.

23.

The **PA-7530** is Palo Alto's firewall magnum opus. It's raw power wrapped in elegance, driven by intelligence, and honed for war. It doesn't just protect networks—it **elevates** them. If the PA-220 is a security ninja, the PA-7530 is a cybernetic kaiju with a mission. It isn't afraid of threats—it **hunts** them. And when it finds them, it doesn't just block them. It **erases them from history**, with logs to prove it.